The reign of grace

The reign of grace

Abraham Booth

EVANGELICAL PRESS

EVANGELICAL PRESS
Faverdale North Industrial Estate, Darlington, DL3 0PH, England

Evangelical Press USA
P. O. Box 84, Auburn, MA 01501, USA

e-mail: sales@evangelicalpress.org

web: http://www.evangelicalpress.org

First published 2003

British Library Cataloguing in Publication Data available

ISBN 0 85234 527 5

Printed and bound in Great Britain by Creative Print and Design Wales, Ebbw Vale, South Wales.

Contents

Preface

The reign of grace has much to commend it to the people of God in this generation. As I was updating Booth's classic work, I was impressed with it in various ways:

1. *The reign of grace* is thoroughly scriptural. We do not find the thoughts and ideas of man presented in these pages but a true exposition of the Word of God. Booth is 'full of Scripture', as you will see. He wants to base everything he says fairly and squarely on the text of the Bible.

2. This book truly glorifies God and his grace. The most wonderful thing about the doctrines of grace is that they give all the glory for our salvation to God alone. This work on grace is no exception. Booth's great passion is to glorify God, and it is the constant theme of this book.

3. You will also be struck with the warmth and fervour of Booth's writing. In fact, his passion and vigour may sound strange to modern ears and come across as somewhat harsh. However, this book was written by a man who had a burning love for Christ and devotion to the Word of God. This is not a dry and dusty theological volume but experimental Calvinism at its very best. Here is a work to fire our love for

Jesus and to stir our hearts, especially when we are going through a time of spiritual deadness or coldness. Abraham Booth is on fire for God in this book and he wants us to be as well. For this reason I believe *The reign of grace* can be used devotionally. In other words, if you prayerfully read a few pages each day, savouring the wonderful truths Booth presents, you will find your mind informed, your will directed and your heart stirred. I also believe that the passion and directness of these pages is an example of what preaching should be like if we are called to declare God's truth. Bland and passionless preaching is nothing less than a tragedy. Booth's very style has something to teach us.

4. Booth has no difficulty in asserting the doctrines of grace with vigour whilst appealing to sinners to be saved. With C. H. Spurgeon and John Murray, Abraham Booth believed that the doctrines of grace could, and indeed should, be preached winsomely in an evangelistic context. In our day there is a seeming reluctance to preach the gospel from any text that savours of 'Calvinism', in the fear that unbelievers will be put off. Sadly, the doctrines of grace are rarely taught to believers either. Booth sees these doctrines as being relevant for both unbelievers and believers.

5. *The reign of grace* also touches on at least two present areas of confusion in Christian doctrine. You will notice that there are two separate chapters dealing with forgiveness and justification. Rightly, Booth saw these as inseparable and yet distinct acts of grace. Very often today, justification is merely seen as forgiveness and not a declaration of God based on the imputation of Christ's righteousness. Secondly, Booth shows in a wonderful way how the doctrines of grace should influence and motivate us in holy living. I think it

striking to even have a chapter entitled 'The reign of grace in our *sanctification*'. We do not tend to connect grace with the duties and responsibilities of Christian living. Booth insists that grace leads to holiness and has strong words for those who believe and even defend the doctrines of grace whilst living in pride and ungodliness. In fact, Abraham Booth's original purpose in writing this book was to humble the pride of men and to show that grace, when rightly understood and embraced, leads to a life of love and holiness.

It has been a great privilege to be involved with the re-publication of a work so highly prized by men such as Thomas Chalmers and John Murray, among many others. My prayer and hope is that it will be read and be a blessing to all Christians. This updated edition of *The reign of grace* is within the reach of any believer with a serious mind who wants to 'grow in grace and in the knowledge of our Lord and Saviour Jesus Christ' (2 Peter 3:18). For these reasons, I have kept Booth's original footnotes to an absolute minimum so as not to make this new edition overly long. In the original work, Booth does quote from a few other authors in the footnotes, most notably John Owen and Jonathan Edwards. Happily, as a Calvinistic Baptist, Abraham Booth stood in the theological tradition of the Reformers and Puritans. I would wholeheartedly direct the reader to the writings of these other men of God for further help in doctrinal understanding and practical -Christian living.

I would like to thank my wife Rachel for her support and encouragement in the updating and editing of this book. I am also grateful to the members of my former fellowship, Harrold and Carlton Grace Baptist Church, for allowing me the time for this project. They love the doctrines contained in this book. I would also like to thank Jackie Friston of Evangelical Press for her hard work in editing my update of Booth and especially for providing the subheadings within each chapter and a Scripture index, both of which greatly enhance the value of this book.

May the God of all grace bless this volume to you.

Richard Inns
Handbridge, Chester

The reign of grace

Chapter 1

The meaning of the term 'grace'

'Never forget that
grace is either
absolutely free or it is
not grace at all.'

1.
The meaning of the term 'grace'

In order to proceed with the greatest clarity and certainty in our study of this subject, it is necessary to consider what is implied by the term *grace*. The primary and principal meaning of the word is 'free favour or unmerited kindness'. This is how it is most frequently used in God's inspired Word, and is how it is to be understood in the words of the Holy Spirit under consideration. In the writings of Paul, grace stands in direct opposition to works and worthiness of every kind and of every degree. This is seen in the following passages of Scripture: 'Now to him who works, the wages are not counted as grace but as debt' (Rom. 4:4). 'Therefore it is of faith that it might be according to grace' (Rom. 4:16). 'For by grace you have been saved ... not of works, lest anyone should boast' (Eph. 2:8-9). 'Who has saved us ... not according to our works, but according to his own purpose and grace' (2 Tim. 1:9).

Presupposes unworthiness

Just as the word mercy, in its primary meaning, relates to a creature in a condition of suffering, so grace, in its proper and strict meaning, always presupposes unworthiness in its object. We realize, then, that whenever anything precious is given to any of Adam's apostate children by the blessed God, it must be

through grace, since those who receive such blessings are unworthy of them. As soon as any degree of worth appears, grace
ceases to reign and justice takes over. Therefore, grace and
worthiness cannot be joined together with the same purpose in
mind. The one must necessarily give place to the other, in accordance with the following remarkable verse of Scripture: 'And
if by grace, then it is no longer of works; otherwise grace is no
longer grace. But if it is of works, it is no longer grace; otherwise work is no longer work' (Rom. 11:6). The apostle's reasoning is very clear: whatever is of works is not of grace at all and
whatever is of grace is not in any way of works. In Paul's view,
works and grace are essentially opposite and as irreconcilable
as light and darkness. When Paul presents the wonderful blessings of salvation as flowing from divine grace, we are led to
consider the people to whom they are given. Not only do they
have no claim to these blessings but they deserve quite the
reverse. They have brought upon themselves a dreadful curse
and are justly exposed to eternal ruin.

Is eternal and free

Therefore, the grace with which we are dealing may be defined
as 'the eternal and unconditional free favour of God which is
manifested in the certain bestowal of spiritual and eternal blessings to the guilty and unworthy'. We shall show what these
blessings are in the following pages. Before that, we should
note that according to this definition, the grace of God is eternal. This concurs with those encouraging words found in the
prophecy of Jeremiah: 'Yes, I have loved you with an everlasting love' (Jer. 31:3). It is divinely free and infinitely rich. This
grace had nothing to do with any claim of human worth. It
operates independently of anything that may be performed by
men and women. It is superior to human guilt, superabounding

over all human unworthiness. Such is the eternal origin and the glorious basis of our salvation! In the same way, it proceeds and is carried on to perfection. Grace shines through the whole of salvation. One writer describes it beautifully as being 'not like a fringe of gold, bordering a garment; it is not like an embroidery of gold, decorating a robe; but it is like the mercy-seat of the ancient tabernacle, which was pure gold throughout'.

For his glory

Do you realize that this is the inexhaustible source of all those priceless blessings that the Lord gives to his unworthy creatures, both in this world and in the next? The Lord's intention, in all that he does or will ever do for sinners, is to make his grace eternally glorious in their eyes and in the eyes of all his holy angels. The indelible motto inscribed by the hand of Jehovah on all the blessings of the unchangeable covenant is, 'To the praise of the glory of his grace' (Eph. 1:6).

In conclusion

By its very definition grace, as it is worked out in our salvation, is in direct opposition to all works and worthiness. We discover from this that those who seek to join grace and works together are terribly deceived. They may make high claims concerning their own holiness of life. However, it is clear from the Word of God and from the very nature of grace that they are on a road that will certainly lead to the everlasting ruin of their souls. Perhaps grace will prevent this, that very grace of which they have such false and corrupt ideas. Divine grace disdains the assistance of men and women's poor and imperfect efforts in the work of salvation. This is the exclusive right of grace alone. Any attempt to complete what grace begins betrays our pride, offends the Lord and cannot be for our spiritual advantage. Never forget that grace is either absolutely free or it is not grace at all. Never forget that anyone who professes to be saved by grace must believe in his heart that he is saved entirely by that grace. If he does not, then he is being inconsistent in matters of the greatest importance.

The reign of grace

Chapter 2

The reign of grace in the whole of our salvation

'Sovereign grace lifts the poor and needy out of the dust and sets them on thrones of glory among the princes of heaven.'

2.
The reign of grace in the whole of our salvation

Grace, in our text, is compared to a sovereign. A sovereign is invested with royal power and the highest authority. It follows that grace, in her kind rule, must exert and manifest sovereign power. She must take over the reign and nullify the mighty influences of sin. Unless this happens, grace cannot bring the sinner to eternal life. In the Scriptures, the Holy Spirit also compares sin to a sovereign, but this reign ends in death.

Displays supreme compassion

Sin is a sovereign who is dreadfully perverted and who is armed with a power that destroys sinners, bringing physical death upon them and threatening them with the everlasting flames of hell. Grace is seen on the throne, adorned in the beauties of holiness and smiling with divine kindness. She feels the tenderest compassion and is armed with a tremendous power that cannot be resisted. Grace is absolutely determined to exert her authority and fulfil her desire to show compassion. She will always do so under the guidance of infinite wisdom in order to bring everlasting glory to God's inflexible justice, sacred truth and all of his other perfect attributes. Grace delivers condemned sinners from the jaws of destruction and speaks peace to those whose consciences are distressed. She bestows a supreme love for God and a delight in the ways of holiness upon those who had departed from God and offended him. To crown all of this, she brings them in safety to the eternal glory and joys of heaven. In summary, the heart of this mighty sovereign is pure compassion, her looks are love, her words are as soothing ointment to the bleeding soul and her arm is salvation. This is the kind of sovereign she is. All who are delivered by her enjoy a complete salvation and are supremely happy as they live under her kind rule.

Always completes her work

As she reigns in our salvation, divine grace is majestic and triumphant. She provides freely everything that is necessary for our eternal happiness. Grace does not save by lowering God's standards to accommodate the weaknesses of fallen creatures but begins, continues and completes the arduous work herself. She does not rescue the sinner from deserved ruin and then give him a new inward power, only to leave him to resist the devil, put to death indwelling sin and live a holy life all alone. Such holiness is essential as a preparation for his now rightful place in heaven. If a sinner was left to find his own way like this, then matters of the greatest importance concerning God's glory and man's happiness would be very uncertain. It would also lead to spiritual pride and give room for boasting. But these things are completely contrary to the honour of the Most High and would frustrate the noble purposes of grace. This wonderful favour is not satisfied with merely laying the foundation but builds the structure as well. Grace not only begins salvation but also brings it to completion. In the parable that Jesus told, the Pharisee, in a way, acknowledged God's grace in his life because he said, 'God I thank you... ' (Luke 18:11). Yet, it is clear that his views of grace were very narrow and his hopes were misplaced. If we view grace as reigning, we must view it as the alpha and omega, the beginning and the end of our salvation. In this way the God of all grace will receive all the glory for his greatest of works.

How do you view God's wonderful grace? Do you realize that you are, by nature, under the dreadful reign of sin in terms of its guilt and power? The apostle Paul teaches us that *sin* reigns (Rom. 5:21). The reign of sin, if grace does not intervene, ends in eternal death. How can you sleep your life away and dream of being happy in heaven, while under the dominion of such an evil ruler? Will the trivialities of this passing world amuse you, when your undying soul is at stake? If this is so, then you are in a pitiful and dreadful condition. Wake up! Get up! Bow your knee to divine grace while she still holds out to you the golden sceptre of pardon and peace. Acknowledge her supremacy and submit to her government, before justice sits on the throne and the arrows of God's vengeance are sent forth. All opportunity to be saved by grace will then be at an end. Even though you cry out for mercy, you will not be heard.

Can save the worst sinner

Perhaps your conscience has been awakened to the need of salvation, but you think that you can save yourself. You have no strength to do this and grace is not intended to help weak, but well-meaning, sinners to effect their own deliverance. The mercy of God and the gospel of Christ were never designed to assist and reward the righteous but to help the miserable and save those who are desperate, those who can do nothing to save themselves. If you were aware of the reign of sin in your life and that the only hope of escape is through reigning grace, you would cry out for help and grace would intervene to save you.

If you are burdened with a sense of sin and disturbed with a
fear of being cast into hell, if you are aware of the sinfulness of
your heart and of the many iniquities in your life, if you realize
that your best efforts are defective and you feel your unworthiness, if you are about to sink into despondency, then remember that *grace* is on the throne. This forbids despair. Grace reigns,
not because God's justice has been compromised, not because
the law has been dishonoured, but because the Lamb has shed
his blood. Grace reigns on the basis of the perfect obedience
and atoning death of the Son of God. In this way, she is highly
exalted. The very worst of sinners may have free access to this
compassionate and kind sovereign. Grace is able to meet the
greatest possible needs quickly and easily. The fact that grace is
enthroned proclaims that the most serious acts of wickedness
are not a barrier to any sinner who wants to come to Christ for
salvation. It is amazing to think that the unworthy and sinful
are, in fact, the only people whom grace is concerned to help!

In conclusion

Do you feel your need and know your pitiful state? Then you
may come freely for salvation. Jehovah has seen your poor
condition and has planned your complete deliverance by
erecting this wonderful throne of grace. You alone have a right
of access to this mercy-seat. If only sinners really knew their
true spiritual condition and the glory of grace! How they would
crowd around this mighty sovereign! With longing hearts, im-
ploring hands, full of expectancy and being sure of success,
they would throng her courts. Sin brings everyone down to the
same level and so sinners from every part of society, who feel
their need, can have free access to this bountiful sovereign.
Before the throne of grace there is no difference between the
morally upright, the outwardly religious and the very worst of

criminals. In God's sight we are all criminals and we are all under the same condemnation. The only hope we have is contained in the compassionate proclamations that come from the throne of grace and are found in the Scriptures (Isa. 45:1-3; Matt. 11:28; John 6:37; 7:37; Rev. 22:17). These proclamations of grace come to the worst offenders and declare that there is pardon for the most heinous of sins. These afford encouragement to the vilest sinner living, to receive immediately God's blessing of salvation and, with gratitude, to rejoice in his grace. Sovereign grace lifts the poor and needy out of the dust and sets them on thrones of glory among the princes of heaven. May we all remember these things so that we might be comforted and encouraged.

I have sought to show how grace reigns in the whole of our salvation. In the following chapters, I will show how grace reigns in our election, calling, pardon, justification, adoption, sanctification and perseverance to eternal life. These are the essential parts of our salvation and in them all, grace reigns in a powerful and glorious way.

The reign of grace

Chapter 3

The reign of grace in our election

'Election is the first
link in the golden chain
of our salvation and the
cornerstone in the
amazing fabric of
human happiness.'

3.
The reign of grace in our election

Many blessings flow from God's sovereign goodness and reigning grace. The first of these that we ought to consider is election. The grace of our glorious King was first manifested in choosing Christ as the head, and in him, everyone who would ever be saved as his members. Therefore, election is the first link in the golden chain of our salvation and the cornerstone in the amazing fabric of human happiness.

For his own glory

Jehovah existed before creation and he is the one who upholds and rules the universe. The purpose for which God does anything is always his own glory. This is because he is infinite and perfect. Even before creation and the beginning of time, the adored Creator was determined to manifest his glory. This was his supreme purpose when he brought everything into existence by the word of his power. Everything was created with this end in view. The highest seraph that surrounds the throne of heaven and the lowest insect that crawls in the dust are both created by God and, in different ways, glorify the Creator. To suggest that the perfect God created the universe for any other purpose is to detract from the honour of the one who is the source of everything.

In man

The noblest part of God's creation in this world was man himself when first formed by the hands of his Maker. Man was made in the image of the great Creator and was endowed with the highest powers and abilities. He was especially created to serve the purposes of God's glory. The entrance of sin into the world did not overthrow this wonderful purpose but was, in fact, part of God's plan to glorify himself. It is impossible for sin to frustrate God's great purpose, which was formed by his own boundless wisdom. In the Scriptures we learn that God knows all his works from before creation itself (Acts 15:18).

In sin

Men and women often regard events as being uncertain or as happening by chance, but every event is absolutely certain to the one who is perfect in knowledge. The entrance of sin, whether among men or angels, cannot in any way frustrate the purposes of Jehovah. 'My counsel shall stand, and I will do all my pleasure' (Isa. 46:10). The fall of mankind into sin was a terrible event because through it, all of Adam's children were defiled and ruined. Yet we know from God's own revelation that he declares 'the end from the beginning' (46:10). Therefore, he not only foresaw all this, but also planned, from eternity, to reveal his perfect character and to be glorified by it. God's plan was to glorify himself both in the full salvation and endless happiness of some from among fallen humanity, and in the just condemnation of others. In this way, the great God is glorified continually by all mankind. For example, God is glorified even by the proud king of Egypt who refused to submit to him with these words: 'Who is the LORD that I should obey his voice?' (Exod. 5:2). God was also glorified by David, the king of Israel, the 'man after [God's] own heart' (1 Sam. 13:14). We could say the same about Judas, who betrayed the Lord Jesus, and about Paul, who was so faithful and was even prepared to die with joy, if it would bring honour to his Saviour. Just as David and Paul are monuments of sovereign grace, so the king of Egypt and Judas are monuments of God's righteous vengeance. In all of them God will be glorified for all eternity to come. As Jehovah is absolutely sovereign, he is completely free to do what he likes with his creatures who have offended him, in any way that will bring him glory. To dispute this is to deny his divine sovereignty and, like Pharaoh, to refuse to submit to his lordship.

God created Adam with the freedom to exercise his own will and knew that he would choose to sin. In the light of this, God, out of free distinguishing love, chose a certain number from fallen humanity and appointed them to receive grace in this life, and to enjoy glory in the life to come. In carrying out this plan, God has acted in a way that is consistent with, and to the glory of, his own excellent character. This is how we define God's gracious act of election, the subject of this chapter.

Opposition to election

The doctrine of election, or as we sometimes call it, the doctrine of distinguishing grace, is rejected and ridiculed today. It is not thought to be worth any serious thought by many who are sophisticated in their thinking. In times past, great men who were noted for their piety and learning always gave a prominent place to this doctrine in their theological works. This was especially true of the early Reformers who delivered the church from the darkness of Roman Catholicism. Election is now considered to be a relic from the past which gullible men believed hastily. It is dismissed as a teaching that is abhorrent to human reason and even opposed to God's perfect character. It is thought best to forget all about election as something that we should not presume to pry into, as it is a waste of time. This doctrine is slandered because it is considered to be detrimental to practical godliness and the happiness and hope of mankind. No wonder election has become so out of fashion today.

It reveals our pride

Why is there so much opposition to this teaching? The reason must be because it lays the axe to the root of all our supposed moral excellence about which we love to boast. One of the main purposes of election is that it is designed to reveal all hidden pride within the heart. Everyone is brought down to the same level. The only reason why God should choose one person for salvation and not another is revealed in the words of our Lord: 'Even so, Father, for so it seemed good in your sight' (Matt. 11:26). Everyone who believes and loves this doctrine rests upon this. So we must resolve any difficulties that we have with election, by leaving the matter with the sovereign God. The Word of God has no praise for anyone who would dare to call God to account over this matter. This includes those who may be educated, wise and morally upright. The Scriptures oppose such audacity bluntly: 'But indeed, O man, who are you to reply against God?' (Rom. 9:20).

It reveals our works as futile

A further reason why election is opposed is because it teaches that the same sovereign grace which began the work of salvation must also carry on that work to completion. At no point is there a place for any contribution from us. The Most High is always jealous of his own honour and he is determined to have all the glory. For these and other reasons we can see why election is resented and attacked. Men and women rely upon themselves and this independent spirit within them is stirred up by such a teaching. It follows that the few who have lovingly bound themselves to this precious doctrine will be criticized and ridiculed and may even suffer something worse. Such is the unpopularity of this teaching!

I do not intend to give a detailed defence of election in this chapter. I will leave that to those friends of the truth who have more time and greater gifts. In fact, others have already done this and have benefited the church of God. My purpose is to look at the main aspects of this article of the Christian faith and then to support it with some clear and relevant arguments. After this I will consider some ways in which it can be of practical use to us.

A particular people

It is very clear from the inspired Scriptures that those who are called the 'elect' cannot include all of mankind. It is obvious that the 'elect' must be distinguished from others. The very term implies that not all of mankind are chosen. To 'elect' and to 'choose' is the same thing. Whenever any choice is made it follows that something is left out of that choice. This is the general teaching of Scripture: 'I do not speak concerning all of you. I know whom I have chosen' (John 13:18). 'I chose you out of the world' (John 15:19). 'The elect have obtained it, and the rest were blinded' (Rom. 11:7).

The elect should always be thought of as individuals rather than a collective body of people. This is clear from what we find written about them in the infallible rule of our faith and practice. We are taught that their *names are written in heaven* and *in the book of life* and that they are *ordained to eternal life* and *chosen for salvation*. Fully aware of the status and privileges of the elect, the apostle Paul asks the following question in the boldest possible manner: 'Who shall bring a charge against God's elect?' (Rom. 8:33).

It does not require very much learning to realize that these things cannot describe nations, churches or communities in and of themselves. On the contrary, these verses strongly imply that the elect are particular people, whose names are known to God in a special way, as they are the objects of his love, for ever precious to him. They also teach us that election relates to spiritual blessings and the everlasting enjoyments of heaven.

Not all are saved

We can show that the elect are particular people in the following way. From the very beginning, Jehovah's purpose was to manifest his love in saving sinners. It is clear that only a part and not all of mankind are saved. Many are in hell already. If God had chosen everyone for salvation then it means that he has been frustrated in his plan; but this is impossible. This salvation was to be accomplished by God's own Son as the Mediator and Surety. As Mediator and Substitute for sinners, he was to obey, shed his blood and die under the curse of God because of the human guilt imputed to him (2 Cor. 5:21; Gal. 3:13). Just who did the Lord Jesus do all of this for? Who did God plan to save through the death of his Son? Whoever it was, as opposed to others they must have been well known to him. Are we really prepared to suggest that Christ should be a substitute for sinners, be obedient and pour out his precious blood, lay down his life as a ransom to satisfy God's justice, for people who were unknown to him? In the legal world a solicitor does not undertake to help a client without knowing something about him and his situation. Others, who may even be in similar circumstances and require the same kind of help, remain completely unknown to him. Any official documents involved in the case must bear the client's name if they are to become valid.

Elect are certainly saved

God's purpose in saving sinners through the incarnation and death of his own Son could not have been accomplished with absolute certainty apart from election. Let us suppose that his intention was for his Son to die for those who would in time believe in him but without first actually choosing them to that end. This would make it very uncertain whether anyone would ever be saved. Left to themselves, sinners will always prefer unbelief. The only way that God could be sure that anyone would believe was to first choose them. There is nothing certain either in the present or future apart from the sovereign will of God, and this is especially true of the salvation of sinners. If, then, God decreed that some would believe, it means that every one of the elect, without exception, was included in that decree. It is not that God merely foresaw who would believe, because faith is the gift of God and is given only to those to whom he decides to give it. We may safely conclude that, just as the death of Christ was absolutely certain because of God's purpose and the everlasting covenant between the persons of the Trinity, so all those individuals who would ever be saved through Christ's work were chosen by God, set apart from others and committed to the special care of the great Shepherd.

Saved from the beginning of time

It is also clear that the elect were chosen by God before the beginning of time, as election is one of the first effects of his love. God's love is from everlasting and so his love to the elect, in choosing them to perfect happiness, must be eternal. If at any point in the past ages of eternity the blessed God had no thoughts of a Mediator and no plan to reveal his love to miserable and guilty creatures, then it could be assumed that there was a time when the elect were not the objects of his choice. However, we know that from eternity it was the purpose of the triune God — Father, Son and Holy Spirit — to save sinners. From eternity the Mediator was appointed as the one who would accomplish this great salvation. We can, therefore, conclude that those who were to benefit from the work of Christ were also appointed to this salvation from eternity. It is not reasonable to think, and God's revelation forbids such a thought, that the Son of the blessed God would bind himself as Mediator and die as a substitute for those whom he did not know. It is not God's way to act with any such uncertainty. It would be equally wrong of us to think that any of God's plans do not date from eternity because he is eternal and infinite in knowledge. This is especially true of redemption as the very greatest of his works.

The words of the Holy Spirit found in the Scriptures prove this point. We read: 'God from the beginning chose you for salvation' and 'He chose us in him before the foundation of the world' (2 Thess. 2:13; Eph. 1:4). They were chosen in Christ as their head and representative. Christ and the elect form one spiritual body. He is the head and they are the members, 'the fulness of him who fills all in all' (Eph. 1:23). The emphatic statement 'before the foundation of the world' clearly refers to eternity. Time did not exist before the universe was created. Before creation there was no time, as we understand it, only a timeless eternity. In the same letter, the same writer, when speaking of the amazing plan of man's redemption which was formed in God's mind, calls it the 'eternal purpose, which he accomplished in Christ Jesus our Lord' (Eph. 3:11). As we have already seen, this must include the choosing of those who are to be redeemed.

Prepared for heaven

This truth may also be proved by considering the fact that the glory of heaven was prepared before the foundation of the world for those who would inherit it. It follows that the grace and spiritual blessings needed to make them ready for heaven were given to them in Christ Jesus at the same time. These blessings were placed into his hands, as their covenant Head and appointed Mediator, for their benefit, before the world began (2 Tim. 1:9; Eph. 1:3-4). As God is eternal and infinite in knowledge we cannot suppose, for one moment, that any of his plans were not from everlasting. To do so would mean that we believe his knowledge to be defective and his perfect attributes prone to change. Such suggestions are completely unworthy of the one whose name is Jehovah.

Chosen by sovereign grace

Can we think of any reason why the elect were chosen to receive life and glory, while others were left in their sins to perish under the punishment of divine justice? No reason can be found in mankind itself because every individual is seen by God as being in exactly the same condition. Yet, the Author of all things and Lord of the world has condescended to give us a reason in his Word. He says, 'I will have mercy on whomever I will have mercy' (Rom. 9:15). Our adored Redeemer gave his assent to this when he spoke these remarkable words: 'Even so, Father, for so it seemed good in your sight' (Matt. 11:26). The great apostle Paul, who was caught up to the third heaven, also rested entirely on God's sovereignty (Rom. 11:15-16). This is where we should all rest, without a word of complaint or any opposition in our minds. It is impossible to rebel against the Most High in the matter of his sovereign will and not be guilty in his sight. Those who continue in such rebellion will not escape his punishment.

   It has been suggested that the elect were chosen by the all-knowing God because he foresaw their faith, holiness and obedience; and that they would persevere to the end. It was these qualities that moved God to set his love on them. Is this correct? Not at all. Grace reigns in the choice of all the elect and, as a sovereign, scorns every proud attempt to usurp her position. She never smiles on anyone because they think them-selves worthy. She never honours anyone because they are better than others. To do this would be very inconsistent with her lovely character and would completely overthrow her won-derful intention. Grace always acts with the condescension of an absolute sovereign in bestowing her favours on her subjects. Wherever she grants her assistance, it is always for the benefit of those who have no other help or plea. Let us consider the following arguments that prove this point.

Faith follows election

The Spirit of Truth describes faith in Christ and the holy obedi-ence that follows faith as *flowing from* election. It is absurd to think that faith and obedience are the *causes* of election. This would contradict the clear teaching of God's Word. For it is written: 'As many as had been appointed to eternal life be-lieved' and 'He chose us ... that we should be holy' (Acts 13:48; Eph. 1:4). They believed because they were 'appointed to eter-nal life'. They were not appointed to eternal life because it was foreseen that they would believe. They were not chosen be-cause they were holy or might become holy. They were chosen in order to make them holy. The only ones who ever believe are those whom God calls by his grace. The only ones whom God calls are those who were predestined to be conformed to the image of Christ. As Paul says: 'Whom he predestined, these he also called' (Rom. 8:30). Furthermore, we know that those whom God chooses are Christ's sheep. According to the words of Christ himself, only his sheep ever believe in him: 'But you do not believe, because you are not of my sheep' (John 10:26). These words teach us that believing does not make us, nor give us a right to be, Christ's sheep. Believing in Christ shows that we were already considered as sheep by God and that we had already been committed to the care of the great Shepherd, so that he might save us. Consider God's Word further: 'God, who has saved us and called us with a holy calling, not according to our works, but according to his own purpose and grace which was given to us in Christ Jesus before time began' (2 Tim. 1:8-9). Here we are taught that we were not called because of our past or future works but because of the everlasting purpose and free distinguishing grace of the one who 'works all things according to the counsel of his will' (Eph. 1:11). It is clear, therefore, that we were not chosen because God foresaw our faith and holiness.

To confirm this, it is important to realize that faith and holiness, in the plan of grace, have a middle position. They are not the foundation, neither are they the roof of this spiritual building. Faith and holiness are inseparable from election but they are neither its cause nor its consummation. The cause of election is sovereign grace. The consummation of election is eternal glory. Someone has compared faith and holiness to the stalk of a plant which draws up the nutrients from the roots in order for there to be fruit. The stalk is neither the roots nor the fruit. So we read in the Scriptures: 'For by grace you have been saved *through* faith' and 'God ... chose you for salvation *through* sanctification by the Spirit and belief in the truth' (Eph. 2:8; 2 Thess. 2:13). If we plan to do something, the cause of that plan is our own will and not the means that we will use to carry out that plan. Besides, why should God choose to save those who already had faith and holiness? What then is the point of election? It is, therefore, ridiculous to say that the cause of election is our faith and works.

According to God's pleasure

Election depends upon the mere good pleasure of God and not anything in us that might influence his will. No other reason

is given by Paul when he states and defends this doctrine and
no other reason is given by his Lord. Paul tells us that the immortal King 'predestined us ... according to the good pleasure
of his will' (Eph. 1:5). He says that it is 'not of him who wills,
nor of him who runs, but of God who shows mercy' and that
'he has mercy on whom he wills' (Rom. 9:16, 18). The Lord
Jesus said with joy, 'I thank you, Father, Lord of heaven and
earth, that you have hidden these things from the wise and
prudent and have revealed them to babes. Even so, Father, for
so it seemed good in your sight' (Matt. 11:25-26). These verses
all relate to the outworking of God's purpose in election.

Christ is the Wisdom of God and has an intimate knowledge of the counsels of heaven. The only reason he gives as to
why the mysteries of the gospel are revealed to some, while
others, who have greater abilities and reputations in the world,
are left in ignorance in order to increase their guilt and condemnation, is the sovereign pleasure of the one who 'does not
give an accounting of any of his words' (Job 33:13).

The words of Paul, when he defends the doctrine of divine
election, are relevant to our argument. With Jacob and Esau in
mind he says: 'For the children not yet being born, nor having
done any good or evil, that the purpose of God according to
election might stand, not of works but of him who calls' and
'The older shall serve the younger' (Rom. 9:11-12). From this
we learn that, before they were born, Jacob and Esau had not
done anything to earn either God's favour or his disapproval.
Yet God chose one and not the other. This is one example of
God's way of working in all mankind. Again Paul says: 'There
is a remnant according to the election of grace' (Rom. 11:5).

The opposite nature of grace and works

He backs up this statement by the following powerful argument, which is from the very nature of grace as opposed to
works: 'And if by grace, then it is no longer of works; otherwise

grace is no longer grace. But if it is of works, it is no longer grace; otherwise work is no longer work' (Rom. 11:6). Nothing could be plainer or asserted with more vigour. Let us, then, submit our minds and consciences to the clear words of the infallible Spirit given through the Lord's ambassador. Paul teaches and proves that our election to eternal glory must either be all of grace or all of works because grace and works are completely opposite. Grace and works cannot unite in saving us. It must be the one or the other. It follows that if we believe that we have been chosen for future happiness in heaven, we must consider the basis of that choice either to be because we were better than others (grace having nothing to do with it, as it was something which we deserved as of right) or because of sovereign grace, we being as unworthy of it as those who perish in hell.

If there is another alternative, then the Apostle's argument cannot stand up. It is impossible to reconcile grace and works in the scheme of salvation. Men, in their pride, may try but they will fail. To attempt it creates confusion because the distinction between grace and works becomes blurred. There are those who say that election is all of grace but then claim that God chose his people because he foresaw their faith and obedience. On this basis election is not of grace at all because grace is free favour. Election then becomes God rewarding sinners for their good works which he foresaw they would do and which they deserved as of right. To think of election in this way is to turn the idea and clear meaning of grace on its head.

Objections to the doctrine of election answered

In his letter to the Romans, it is Paul's chief purpose to prove that election excludes any thought of human worth and to show that it is all of God's free and sovereign grace. He answers all sorts of objections. The Apostle's opponents claim that election

must have been on the basis of the greater worth of those who
were chosen or else God would have been grossly unfair. After
dealing with God's distinguishing love to Jacob and rejection
of Esau, Paul begins to meet the objections that arise within the
heart. He anticipates the charge of unfairness in this way: 'What
shall we say then? Is there unrighteousness with God? Certainly
not!' (Rom. 9:14). Is there anyone who would dare to say that
God is unrighteous because he bestows or withholds his favours
according to his own sovereign pleasure? All who revere their
Maker abhor such a thought.

No merit in those saved

After rejecting such a shocking inference in the strongest way
possible, Paul then goes on to confirm and prove his doctrine
by appealing to the words of Jehovah to Moses recorded in the
ancient Scriptures: 'I will have mercy on whomever I will have
mercy, and I will have compassion on whomever I will have
compassion' (Rom. 9:15; Exod. 33:19). In the following verse
he makes this conclusion: 'So then it is not of him who wills,
nor of him who runs, but of God who shows mercy.' This shows
that it was Paul's purpose to prove, not only that some of fallen
humanity have been chosen while others have been passed by,
but also that those who were chosen were no different from
those who were passed by. The Apostle shows that the elect
were appointed to glory according to the good pleasure of God
alone and not because of any claim which they had upon his
mercy. This is why he writes as he does, not to lead us into
error, but to establish us in the truth of God's grace in election.

Without fault?

After answering the first objection, Paul is then concerned to
answer another. How zealous and untiring the Apostle was in
maintaining God's truth! He goes on to say, 'You will say to me

then, "Why does he still find fault? For who has resisted his will?"' (Rom. 9:19). The objection here is, that if God is so sovereign in salvation, he cannot find fault with his creatures because they cannot but be in subjection to God and his sovereign purposes. Here is a mirror in which everyone who objects to divine sovereignty may see his face and know his character. Here in summary are the appalling and shocking consequences (it is thought) of the doctrine of eternal, unconditional and personal election.

People today draw the same terrible conclusions but with these words: 'The Calvinistic doctrine of election makes men into machines. They are no longer responsible for their behaviour. They cannot be praised or blamed, rewarded or punished. We might as well say "goodbye" to conduct that is good and worthy of praise. If we are righteous or wicked in this life, saved or damned in the life to come, it is because of an arbitrary will and sovereign, omnipotent decree.' Those who make this worn-out objection ought to think about how Paul refutes it and how he treats those who arrogantly oppose the sovereign rights of the supreme God.

God's right

Although the objection is extremely bold and blasphemous, the Apostle in no way suggests that he was mistaken in declaring that the sovereign pleasure of God is the only reason why some will enjoy eternal glory in heaven and others will suffer the everlasting torments of hell. He again asserts the absolute sovereignty of the Creator of the universe. Rather than tone down what he had already stated, although it might have sounded harsh, he confirms that he was right to have written what he did by declaring again that the Majesty of heaven has an absolute right to dispense his favours as he pleases. Paul desired constantly to see Jehovah glorified and he could in no way deny the God who is above. What does the great Apostle say?

'But indeed, O man, who are you to reply against God?' (Rom. 9:20). Will a worm of the earth, an insect, an atom, call to account the conduct of the Lord of the universe and declare it to be unfair? Shall impotence and dust fly in the face of Omnipotence? Shall corruption and guilt set the rules of fairness by which the Most Holy shall regulate his behaviour regarding the rebellious subjects of his vast empire? May it never be! 'Woe to him who strives with his Maker! Let the potsherd strive with the potsherds of the earth!' (Isa. 45:9). Let not the worthless fragment presume to make war with heaven because the divine wrath, like a devouring fire, might break out and consume it.

Having rebuked the foolishness and pride of the opposer, Paul continues to make his point with an everyday illustration which everyone can understand: 'Will the thing formed say to the one who formed it, "Why have you made me like this?" Does not the potter have power over the clay, from the same lump to make one vessel for honour and another for dishonour?' (Rom. 9:21). Such an assertion is undeniable. If everyone allows this right to a mere potter on earth, then will anyone presume to deny it to the one who formed all things? To deny God this right would be not only wicked but foolish and blasphemous.

The Apostle proceeds to apply this illustration: 'What if God, wanting to show his wrath and to make his power known, endured with much longsuffering the vessels of wrath prepared for destruction, and that he might make known the riches of his glory on the vessels of mercy, which he had prepared beforehand for glory' (Rom. 9:22-23). If God chooses to pour out his wrath upon those who deserve it and to reveal his boundless love in saving others from the destruction which they also deserve, who has the right to complain? Shall the eye of anyone be evil because their offended Maker is good? Does he not have the eternal right to do what he pleases with his own? Is he obliged to explain himself to his creatures? It is acceptable for kings who rule in this world to choose who they will favour and, in certain circumstances, to show mercy to criminals, whilst leaving others to be punished for their crimes. No one would presume to question the authority of the king. Yet so many would seek to question God's right to rule over his subjects! How utterly foolish because God does reign, regardless of what people think or say!

God is wise

God does bestow his favour on whom he pleases, but it is important to realize that all that he does is influenced by his infinite wisdom. He always has the highest reason for doing what he does. Divine sovereignty is not blind favouritism or mere 'will' without the guidance of wisdom. God always does what is wise and right in governing the affairs of his vast empire in order to reveal his own glorious attributes. Otherwise, God's rule would be like that of a cruel dictator. Of course, it is quite wrong to think of God's sovereignty in this way.

It is so crucial to realize that the love of God to his offending creatures is directed by his infinite understanding, knowledge and wisdom. Jehovah is perfect in all of his ways and so he governs with righteousness, punishes with justice and forms his plans with wisdom. Paul concludes the subject of God's eternal predestination with these words: 'Oh, the depth of the riches both of the wisdom and knowledge of God!' (Rom. 11:33). In this way the Apostle shows that God's sovereignty in election is not based on an arbitrary will divorced from wisdom. To believe the opposite is neither scriptural nor reasonable. It would represent the Lord as a tyrant rather than one who alone is wise.

God is a compassionate Father

When we think about the Almighty choosing some of fallen humanity to life and happiness, we are to think of him as a compassionate Father who has mercy upon his unhappy children. If, however, we think of him choosing one person and not another, we are to think of him as a sovereign Lord who bestows his favours as he pleases. Therefore, if we ask the question, 'Why was anyone chosen to salvation when everyone deserved to perish?' the answer is, 'Because the Creator is merciful.' However, if we ask the question, 'Why did God choose Paul and not Judas?' the answer is, 'Because he is the Lord of all and has the right to do as he pleases with what belongs to him.' If this answer will not satisfy those who have difficulty with election, then the Holy Spirit requires them to ask the potter why he, from the same lump of clay, makes vessels for very different uses. He will answer: 'Not because of anything in the clay itself, which is all exactly the same, and has no say in how it will be used, but because of my own free choice.' The potter has a kind of sovereignty over his clay and in the same way mankind is in the hand of God. Shall Jehovah have less of a sovereign control over his offending creatures than a mere potter over his clay? Human reason and God's own revelation forbid such a thought. Therefore, in election we have a glorious manifestation of divine grace in all its freeness towards the vessels of mercy and of the absolute sovereignty of God towards all mankind. We behold electing love with wonder and joy and stand silently in awe of absolute sovereignty as we remember who it is who says, 'Be still, and know that I am God' (Ps. 46:10).

I have shown that election is an act of sovereign grace and I now want to consider the wonderful purpose of the Lord in election. The main purpose is his own eternal glory and, after this, the complete happiness of all his people. We have already seen that the glory of God is the ultimate end of all his eternal counsels and works. This is especially true of the plan to save sinners. Everything that God does is for the 'praise of the glory of his grace' (Eph. 1:6).

His own glory

It is often assumed that God's main purpose in election is the happiness of those whom he chose to save and the misery of those whom he rejected. Is it right to say that God's intention in election was the eternal happiness of some and the everlasting torment of others? To do so is a great mistake, as it presents predestination in a very false and unfavourable way. It implies that God, who is infinitely good, takes delight in the endless sufferings of those whom he made in his own image. There must be a greater and more noble purpose to election. That purpose is God's own glory in the wonderful scheme of salvation. It is highly dishonouring to God to suggest that his main aim in election was the damnation of those who perish and not his own glory in revealing his spotless purity and inflexible justice. It is also dishonouring to God to say that his purpose in election was the happiness of his people and not his own glory in manifesting his grace and other wonderful attributes. By punishing sinners, God shows his opposition to all moral evil, he honours his justice and it is seen that he rules over all. By saving some of his rebellious subjects from the death they deserve, he displays his mercy which, working together with his truth and righteousness, is for his own glory. We conclude, with Paul, that the great purpose of election is to 'make known the riches of [God's] glory on the vessels of mercy' (Rom. 9:23).

By his appointed means

Just as the glory of God is the purpose of his decree of election, so the means that he appointed to bring his chosen ones to eternal happiness are also to his glory and are worthy of his wisdom. The way in which he saves sinners proclaims him to be 'a just God and a Saviour' and that, 'the Lord is righteous in all his ways, and holy in all his works' (Isa. 45:21; Ps. 145:17,

AV). The particular means that God uses to bring his elect to heaven are the incarnation of the eternal Son, his work as the Mediator and the ministry of the Spirit in enabling sinners to believe the truth. We read in the Scriptures: 'For God did not appoint us to wrath, but to obtain salvation through our Lord Jesus Christ' and 'God ... chose you for salvation through sanctification by the Spirit and belief in the truth' (1 Thess. 5:9; 2 Thess. 2:13). Redemption through the blood of Jesus and sanctification through the Spirit of God are essential in the working out of election. There is no forgiveness without the shedding of blood and without holiness no one will see the Lord in glory (Heb. 9:22; 12:14). God punishes sinners in hell because of their own sinful rebellion but he bestows the glory of heaven upon the elect because of the work of Christ *for* them and the ministry of the Holy Spirit *in* them.

In conclusion we can say that, although the work of Christ as Mediator was not the cause of election, yet his obedience and death were essential for the outworking of that great plan of grace. Again, although the Almighty did not choose anyone because he foresaw their faith and obedience, yet in the sovereign decree of election, provision was made for the elect to believe and to live a holy life through the Spirit.

By his unchangeable purposes

God's purpose in election is unchangeable and, therefore, the salvation and everlasting happiness of the elect is absolutely certain. This is clear from the fact that all of God's decrees are unchangeable, including the decree of election. God's Word teaches that his purposes cannot change. For example: 'For the LORD of hosts has purposed, and who will annul it?' (Isa. 14:27); 'My counsel shall stand, and I will do all my pleasure' (Isa. 46:10); 'But he is unique, and who can make him change? And whatever his soul desires, that he does' (Job 23:13); 'To show more abundantly to the heirs of promise the immutability of his counsel' (Heb. 6:17); 'Who has resisted his will?' (Rom. 9:19); 'That the purpose of God according to election might stand' (Rom. 9:11); 'The Father of lights, with whom there is no variation or shadow of turning' (James 1:17).

If God were to change his decrees and alter his purposes it would seriously call into question his omniscience, in that some events were not foreseen by him, and his omnipotence, in that he was not powerful enough to carry out his plans. These things cannot be true of the infinite God whose will determines all events and whose word upholds the universe. If ever God was to change his mind, it must be either for better or for worse. If it was for better, then he was not perfect in the first place. If it was for worse, then he is no longer perfect. People only change their minds because they realize that a previous decision or plan was unwise due to present circumstances that they had not foreseen. To suggest that God is like this is to deny his boundless wisdom and really to deny his deity altogether. Of course, for human beings to change their minds about something can be a very wise thing to do but it still implies that the previous plan was foolish. The God who alone is wise never has second thoughts about anything. He is perfect in wisdom and never has any reason to change his purposes. He is also boundless in his power and is dependent on nobody in carrying out his will. This means that his people will certainly share in those blessings that have been planned for them. To suggest that those whom God has chosen to eternal glory should fall short of enjoying it is ridiculous and irreverent and charges Jehovah with gross imperfection. In doing this we would make God like ourselves in our weakness and fallibility (Ps. 50:21).

Eternal happiness for his people

Election most certainly leads to the eternal happiness of heaven for those whom God chooses. This is seen in the following wonderful passage: 'Whom he predestined, these he also called; whom he called, these he also justified; and whom he justified, these he also glorified. What then shall we say to these things? If God is for us, who can be against us?' (Rom. 8:30-31). Paul shows that God's purpose in election does not change and that it is impossible for those whom God has chosen to fail to reach heaven. The Apostle argues with great certainty that those who were chosen in eternity past will be glorified in the future. This is why he is able to exclaim with such joy and boldness, 'What then shall we say to these things? If God is for us, who can be against us?' Paul would not speak with such certainty and joy if God's purpose could change or his decree could prove weak and be left unfulfilled. The Apostle not only studied under Gamaliel in his younger days but, more importantly, he wrote through the Spirit of wisdom who was giving him these words to write. So from a human and divine perspective we can be sure of the logic of his reasoning and feel the weight of his argument. We can, therefore, be absolutely sure that those God chooses to obtain the future happiness of heaven will certainly obtain it. As Paul says, 'whom he predestined, these he also glorified'. The two cannot be separated.

Election promotes holiness

I want to show now that election is a 'truth according to godliness' (Titus 1:1). What I mean is that election is designed to promote the holiness and happiness of true Christians. As this doctrine is a part of that faith which was once delivered to the saints, it must be beneficial to those who embrace it, in having a sanctifying influence upon them. Those who truly love this aspect of the gospel will find it a friend to their progress in holiness and to their enjoyment of real peace. If it could be proved that election does not lead the saints to holy living and inward peace, then we should abandon it immediately as an error and abhor it as an enemy. All genuine evangelical truth is designed to increase the joy of true Christians and to lead them in ways of holiness. This is certainly true of the doctrine that we are considering. Those who meditate frequently upon election find that their souls are humbled in the dust before the sovereign God, that their hearts are inspired with love towards his wonderful name and that they are filled with gratitude for blessings already received and for all that is yet to come. They find that their holiness and comfort is increased because *humility, love* and *gratitude* are the very life of true religion. If these abound in our hearts, then our spiritual joys are increased and our Maker is glorified. If, however, these graces are declining within us, it will lead to a loss of appetite for the things of God and will have a detrimental effect upon religion generally. Without them the very best religious works and services are of no value at all in God's sight.

Humility

Election is designed to promote genuine humility in us. It teaches that all mankind, in their sinful state, are equally under God's wrath and exposed to eternal ruin, and their condition is absolutely hopeless apart from God's grace in election. This doctrine does not allow anybody to claim proudly that they are better than others. When a Christian thinks of himself more highly than he should he is rebuked sharply with these words: 'For who makes you differ from another? And what do you have that you did not receive? Now if you did indeed receive it, why do you boast as if you had not received it?' (1 Cor. 4:7). Those who are the objects of distinguishing love cannot but lie in humility before God because they realize that they are as sinful as those who finally perish in hell, and the only reason they are saved and others are not is because of sovereign grace.

They always acknowledge that they are the chief of sinners, regarding themselves as worthless in God's sight. They are inwardly humble and this is manifested outwardly in their conduct. When true believers pray to God in the secret place the very language that they use expresses the lowliness of their hearts. In prayer they exalt God and humble themselves. They confess their sins in all of their vileness and acknowledge that they deserve to be cast into hell because of them. They ascribe their salvation to sovereign grace alone and wonder why God should have marked them out for mercy when millions of others are left to perish because of their sins. They plead with God for a heart of humility so that reigning grace might have all the glory.

Love

In a similar way, election inspires a holy love in the hearts of believers. 'God is love, and he who abides in love abides in God, and God in him' (1 John 4:16). In prayer, believers praise God for his electing love and express their amazement that God should have loved them from eternity in spite of their wickedness and rebellion. They ask God to possess their hearts and be the supreme object of their affections. They long that all the idols in their hearts and lives might be thrown down so that the God of all grace can be loved without any rivals.

Gratitude

A right understanding of this glorious truth of election also leads the believer to be filled with gratitude to God. Gratitude is one of those lovely characteristics of the soul. It burns in the hearts of those in glory and is the reason why the heavenly choirs sing praise to God. Love and gratitude are the very essence of all religion, the very life and soul of Christianity. As they are advanced, so the holiness and comfort of mankind are advanced. A warm sense of the election of grace in the heart is a powerful incentive to overflow with thanksgiving to God. As Paul thinks about the riches of grace in election he exclaims: 'Blessed be the God and Father of our Lord Jesus Christ, who has blessed us with every spiritual blessing in the heavenly places in Christ, just as he chose us in him before the foundation of the world' (Eph. 1:3-4). And again: 'But we are bound to give thanks to God always for you, brethren beloved by the Lord, because God from the beginning chose you for salvation' (2 Thess. 2:13). This is how the Apostle expresses his thanks, both for himself and other believers, to the Author of all good for his electing love. Similiar expressions of gratitude will be found in every regenerate heart where election is known and embraced.

The intense desire of believers is to honour God in everything. They are so conscious of how much they owe to God's grace, they devote themselves to him, longing to please him. They pray that they may never bring God's name into disrepute. If they ever do, it causes them pain and distress. They *must* seek the glory of the one who has chosen them to salvation. So we see that election, when rightly understood and believed, always leads to holy living and consecration to God.

Election should not discourage anyone from seeking Christ

It is sometimes argued that, although election is profitable for the believer, it tends to discourage those who show interest in Christian things and fills the convicted sinner with fear. It is thought that election leaves such people wondering whether Christ and his salvation are freely available to them or not. They reason anxiously that if God has not chosen them, then they cannot be saved, however much they desire to be. This objection to election may seem plausible and some may have been troubled by it when seeking salvation, but it is weak and of little weight. It supposes that before a sinner can believe in Christ for salvation, he must know God's eternal purpose for himself, pry into God's sovereign decree and read his own name in the book of life. This is a huge mistake.

Let me give the following illustration. If somebody is hungry and food is given to him, would it be wise and rational for him to hesitate in eating it because he does not know whether his Maker has appointed it especially for him? Would it be right for him not to eat because he is unsure whether in God's providence it will satisfy his hunger? He may well remember that verse: 'Man shall not live by bread alone, but by every word that proceeds from the mouth of God' (Matt. 4:4), and conclude that even if he took it, without God's providence it will do him no good. Surely he would reason in this way: 'Food is given for the benefit of mankind; I feel my need and so I will eat this food in order to satisfy my hunger and sustain my life.' Christ is the bread of life and food for our souls. This spiritual food is provided by grace and is revealed in the gospel. It is offered freely to everyone who hungers, without exception. All that the awakened sinner has to do, with the Lord's help, is to take, eat and live for ever. The gospel is designed for sinners who are starving for lack of spiritual food. The question then for sinners seeking salvation is not: 'Am I one of the elect?' but 'Do I feel my need of Christ?' and if they do, then let them believe upon him and live.

There is the fullest possible provision in the gospel for the sure salvation of every sinner, however unworthy, who feels his need and seeks Christ. When the gospel is preached, sinners are not encouraged to believe in Jesus because they are God's elect but because they are sinners and are ready to perish. All the blessings of grace are available to them for their immediate salvation. All people, without exception and however sinful, who realize their danger and feel their need are invited by the Lord Redeemer to share in spiritual blessings *before* they begin to inquire as to whether God has chosen them or not. The order that has been established in the economy of grace does not require perishing sinners to prove that they are elect before they can trust in Christ for full salvation. If they realize that they are sinners, then Jehovah gives them every encouragement in his Word to rely immediately upon the Saviour. The solemn promise of God assures them that if they believe, then they will know the pardon of their sins, peace in their consciences, freedom from his wrath and the enjoyment of glory in the future. These things are taught clearly in God's revealed Word. To think otherwise is to misunderstand election and, in the end, to abuse the doctrine altogether. It gives no discouragement or reason to fear to those who are aware of their sin and who welcome the good news of a Saviour from the guilt and power of sin. The Redeemer in all his glory, and the gospel with all its blessings, will always be despised by those who are still dead in sin and unconcerned about their souls and by those who trust in their own righteousness for salvation. As the gospel is irrelevant to them, they will never have any genuine concerns about election anyway.

Election should lead to diligence and holiness

It has been suggested that the doctrine of election leads believers to be lazy in their Christian lives and that it actually encourages loose living. Undoubtedly, there are those who profess to believe in election for whom this is true, but they are dreadfully deceived. They abuse election and if they are not careful they will find themselves falling short of the blessing of heaven. I must assert boldly that those who abuse God's grace in this way reveal themselves as vessels of eternal wrath rather

than objects of sovereign mercy. Grace never leads to careless-
ness and sin but has the opposite effect in leading to diligence
and holiness.

This objection would only have some force if it could be
proved that the infinitely wise God has not ordained the means
to bring his elect to glory. To even suggest this would be unworthy of his character and a contradiction of the clear teaching of his Word. It is true that when the sovereign God chose
sinners to salvation, he did not choose them because of anything
in them or because of any good works which he foresaw. Yet,
his purpose in election is stated by Paul: 'just as he chose us in
him before the foundation of the world, that we should be holy
and without blame before him in love' (Eph. 1:4). In the light of
this it is quite astonishing that anyone should think that God's
grace in election is an incentive to gratify their vile lusts! We
might even conclude that God chose sinners so that they could
have even more opportunity and freedom to sin than they would
have had if God had not chosen them! If this is correct then we
should rightly abhor election. However, this is wholly untrue.
We are informed by the oracle of heaven that the objects of
God's grace were chosen for salvation 'through sanctification
by the Spirit and belief in the truth' (2 Thess. 2:13). We can
think of sanctification by the Spirit as the means to bring the
elect to glory and as an essential part of salvation from sin
which is begun on earth and completed in glory. Either way,
Paul's words show that the objection under consideration is
irreverent and completely void of any truth to support it. It follows
that those who make this objection are influenced either by
gross ignorance or by a deep-rooted prejudice. It is clear that
the holiness and happiness of God's people are both made
certain by his purpose in election. It is also true that only those
who live by faith in Jesus Christ and walk in ways of obedience
have any evidence that they are God's elect. Believers can only
have an assurance that they are the objects of God's distinguishing love if they continue to depend upon their glorious

Saviour and walk in paths of holiness. In this way, they will
know much inward peace and spiritual joy.

Election should not discourage the use of means

In salvation

There is another objection to election, which is made frequently
and aggressively. It goes like this: 'If this doctrine is true then
there is no point in using means in order to be saved. If we are
chosen then we will be saved regardless of what we do. If we
are not chosen then anything we do will be in vain. All of our
prayers, tears, striving for holiness, watchfulness and self-denial
are useless. We might just as well take things easy. To profess to
be a Christian is pointless because God has already fixed
everyone's eternal destiny and no one can reverse it.'

This objection is similar to the one we have just considered.
In both cases there is a presumption that God decrees the end
but not the means to that end. This is an obvious error that is
quite absurd. We can see this by applying the same principle to
the everyday affairs of life. God rules in his providence over all
human affairs, however small and insignificant. It is clear from
the Scriptures that the great Ruler of the world decreed all events
before creation, that is, in eternity. An infinite and eternal God
does not make new plans as he goes along. It follows that if this
objection about election is true then it is also true in terms of
our everyday lives. Why exert yourself in order to obtain something good? Why take great pains to avoid some calamity or
disaster? Why bother to go to work? What is the point of eating
a meal and going to sleep at night? The conclusion would be
that 'God has decreed all events so anything that we do is useless. We cannot alter his purpose.'

It is true that God's sovereign purpose stands at all times
and in all circumstances but who, in their right mind, would

draw this conclusion? Only a fool or a madman. We believe in God's eternal decrees. We continually see those decrees worked out in providence. But we never abandon the use of means because of them. What is true of the general affairs of our lives must be especially true of matters relating to salvation, which are infinitely more important. So, in whatever way we think about it, this objection is completely irrational and absurd, being contrary to God's inspired Word and to common sense.

In God's foreknowledge

Not only is this objection opposed to God's sovereign decree, it is also opposed to his infallible foreknowledge. Jehovah's knowledge is perfect, in that it cannot increase. All choices that are ever made by men and women, including the outcome of those choices, were known to God's mind and seen by his omniscient eye in eternity. This means that he foresaw every single event that ever takes place in this world. If then it is said that it is pointless to use means in order to be saved because of the decree of election, the same objection could be made against God's foreknowledge. God's decree and foreknowledge are closely connected and are, in fact, inseparable.

Let me illustrate this point and apply this argument. A man may believe that God's foreknowledge is perfect and yet argue against the use of means like this: 'As the foreknowledge of God is perfect, he saw my final state from eternity. He either saw me seated on a throne of bliss in heaven, praising him for his grace, or loaded down with chains of darkness in hell, groaning because of the agonies of endless despair. Just as God saw me from eternity, so that is where I will be. His foreknowledge is infallible. My eternal state is already fixed in God's mind. It is, therefore, pointless using means either to avoid hell or to obtain heaven. Why should I watch and pray and seek to live the Christian life that is at times so difficult? If the omniscient God foresaw me happy in the future world, I cannot be miserable. If he foresaw me miserable, then I shall not and cannot be happy, though all the angels of heaven and people on earth were to try to help me.'

This is really the same argument that is urged against the decree of election and is, similarly, incorrect and of little weight. Just as Jehovah, when he decreed the end, also decreed the means to that end, so he not only foresaw the end but also the means to that end. Those whom he foresaw in the outer darkness of hell, he also foresaw as being guilty and walking in ways of destruction in this life. Those whom he foresaw in heaven, he also foresaw using the means to that glorious end; means which he himself would make effectual in their lives.

It is clear that those who make this objection must either abandon their argument or deny that their Maker is perfect. In this case, they are robbing God of his deity. Many have, with great irreverence, done just this in order to support their ideas about the freedom of the human will, as opposed to the doctrine of sovereign grace and divine predestination. They know that whoever believes in the eternal and perfect foreknowledge of God cannot consistently deny his decrees concerning the final state of men and women. It has been acknowledged by them that if God has an infallible foreknowledge of all future events, then the predestination of some to life and others to death cannot be refuted. It is terrible to think that they try to prove that he who created and governs the universe does not have such a foresight of future events. In effect, they are saying that he is not God.

Election does not make God guilty of partiality

There is yet another objection that some people make about election: 'This doctrine leads to the conclusion that the Most High deals with his creatures with partiality. It suggests that God treats the greater part of mankind with harshness and injustice, thus making him a respecter of persons.' This charge against God is entirely without foundation. In human affairs the charge of partiality can only be made in the realm of justice; that is, when the rules of fairness are ignored in any situation. However, nobody can be accused of impartiality when they act in the realm of favour and sheer generosity.

Let me illustrate this point. A civil magistrate is invested with official authority by the state to uphold the laws of the land and to administer justice when those laws are broken. Let us suppose that a particular magistrate is very just in inflicting punishment upon the poor people in the land for the crimes that they have committed, whilst allowing the rich to escape punishment for exactly the same crimes. This magistrate would be guilty of partiality and of perverting the course of justice. Then let us consider the same person, not as a magistrate of the state, but as a private person who is very generous to the poor and needy around him. Is he under an equal obligation to help everyone? If he decides to help some and not others, shall we accuse him of being a respecter of persons? Of course not! If this were so, it would mean that those whom he had not helped could come to him and demand that he help them as their right! This would be sheer audacity. So, in election God acts, not as the Judge of all, but as the God of all grace. It has to be said that everybody is obliged to love and assist their neighbour. We are only stewards of what God has given to us and we are accountable to him as to how we use our money, possessions, time and gifts. Yet, God has the absolute right to do what he likes with what belongs to him. No creature, certainly not an offending creature, has the right to demand anything of God by way of his blessing.

If Jehovah must be called a respecter of persons because he loved and chose some to everlasting happiness, while rejecting others and leaving them to perish under his righteous curse, what shall we say about his providence in numerous other instances? Does God not, in spiritual matters, give the means of grace to some people, whilst they are entirely withheld from others? Where the means of grace are enjoyed, does he not regenerate and sanctify some through the Spirit of truth, whilst others, who for example hear the same gospel, continue in spiritual darkness and, in the end, perish in hell? If the sovereign God can do these things for some and not others in time, he can act in a similar way from eternity. In fact, God's providence is the carrying out of his eternal purpose. God acts in the same way in terms of the material blessings that he bestows upon his creatures. It is very clear that the supreme Ruler of the world is generous in giving blessings of every kind to some people, while others, just as sinful and unworthy of anything, are exposed to great hardship all through their lives. It is true that there is a vast difference between material and eternal blessings but, if God is unfair in the one, then he is unfair in the other as well. The Judge of all the earth must do right. Just as no one, without openly blaspheming God, can argue with his sovereignty in matters pertaining to this life, so no one should find fault in the method of his grace in distinguishing between his sinful creatures.

Election does not mean God is unfair

We have shown that election does not make God a respecter of persons but neither can it be said to make him harsh and unfair. Let me ask the objector and let him ask his own conscience: Has all mankind sinned? Is sin a transgression of divine law? Is the law that they have broken righteous in its requirements and just in its penalty? If this is all so, then every person is guilty before God and every mouth should be stopped because all deserve to die and to perish everlastingly in hell. Either these things are true or we must reject the authority of the Bible. God could have left the whole of mankind to perish in hell. If he had done this, it would in no way have been to his dishonour as the sovereign Ruler and righteous Judge. He would have acted in accordance with his justice. In the light of this, how can anyone charge him with harshness and injustice because he chose to save some and reject others? The choice of some in no way injures those who are not chosen. They would not have been any better if none had been chosen, nor any saved. If we can put it like this: non-election is not a punishment; it is simply the withholding of free favour, which the sovereign Lord of all may bestow on anyone, just as he pleases.

When we consider that the whole world is guilty before God, we realize that he has an unlimited right to decide the final state of men and women. God was at perfect liberty to decide to save anyone or not. He could have left everyone to perish; he could have decreed the salvation of everyone. He could have purposed to love and save some, whilst rejecting and punishing others. It is clear that God has the right to leave as few, or as many, to condemnation and wrath as he sees fit. All have sinned, all have forfeited his favour and all deserve to perish. To think otherwise is absurd and quite inconsistent with God's own character. It would mean that those whom he did choose to save had some claim upon his favour above that of others.

It is most appropriate that God should order all things according to his own good pleasure. His infinite greatness, majesty and glory entitle him to act as an absolute sovereign, whose will is carried out in everything. He is worthy, supremely worthy, of making his glory the end of all that he does. In fulfilling his purposes, God never consults his creatures but he always acts in accordance with his own wisdom and will. This is especially true in matters of the greatest importance, such as the salvation and damnation of sinners. It is only right that he should act as the sovereign Lord of heaven and earth. God is eternal and before all things. He is the Creator of the universe, the fountain of all existence and everything is dependent upon him.

If this objection is true, then it would mean that the blessings of grace are not God's to give. It would mean that sinners have a claim upon his mercy. It is ridiculous to speak of *giving* something to anyone if they have a right to it anyway. Were we to apply this to the High and Lofty One, it would mean limiting the exercise of his grace. It would suggest that God does not have the right to bestow his gifts upon those whom he chooses and that, were he to give them to one and not the other, the charge of partiality and cruelty would be made against him. What a shocking thought! The very thought is blasphemous and arises from the high opinions that we have of ourselves and the low thoughts that we entertain of our Maker.

Rejection of fallen angels

It is worth noting that those who make this objection concerning the election of sinners to salvation have no problems with the final rejection of the angels who sinned. In the one case, some of those who sinned were chosen to salvation. In the other, all of those who sinned were condemned to everlasting punishment. Not one fallen angel was chosen for salvation. If some people think that God is somehow dishonoured by the doctrine of election, then how much more in his leaving *all* the angels who fell to suffer his wrath? Yet, we do not find these people pleading the cause of the apostate angels with God and asking him why he did not choose any of them for salvation. They know that the angels deserve to be punished everlastingly and that God's character in this loses nothing of its glory. If this is true of angels, then why not of fallen humanity? If we say that the whole of mankind does not deserve to perish, then we are left with some shocking conclusions: the law of God is unrighteous because it proclaims that sinners must be punished; the death of Christ as a substitute for sinners was an unnecessary and appalling event; the most wonderful parts of the Bible

are unworthy of the least attention; and the distinctive doctrines of Christianity are no better than a dream or fable and
are a gross imposition on those who believe them. If we do not
believe that all of mankind deserve to perish for ever, then there
is no justice in the law and no grace in the gospel. The eternal
integrity of the great Lawgiver and the beauties of our glorious
Saviour are completely obscured. The entire scheme of redemption, as it is revealed in the Scriptures, is overthrown. At the
end of the day, the objector has no alternative but to either
abandon his objection or blaspheme his Maker.

In conclusion

I now want to show how this doctrine of election is profitable to
both the sinner who has no concern for his soul and to the
genuine Christian.

To the sinner

If you are a careless sinner, then election is designed to strike
your conscience, to cause you to feel alarmed and to wake up
your soul so that you begin to seek after eternal happiness. You
now realize that it would be entirely right for God to execute
justice on all who are guilty and that if he had left all mankind
to perish, no one would have any cause for complaint. You
now understand that he has, according to his goodness, chosen
a number of fallen humanity and determined to bring them to
glory, whilst multitudes are left to suffer the terrible penalty of
their crimes. This could be your own awful destiny. Remember
that if you are rejected by God, you are lost for ever.

Are you still unconcerned about your soul? Then the sentence of a broken law and the wrath of an awesome Judge
abide upon you. You are in the hands of an offended God and

how shocking to think that you are uncertain as to what he will do with you. Perhaps you are sometimes afraid that you will receive your due in the lake that burns with fire and brimstone. You have every reason to fear, as long as you go on being careless about your soul and loving pleasure more than God. Your apprehensions over eternal punishment are not without foundation. You have reason to tremble every moment. Remember that eternal punishment is what you deserve.

Your Maker and Sovereign, whom you have offended, may inflict it upon you and still be righteous and holy and actually glorified by it. Remember that your Maker is the sovereign Ruler of the universe and righteous Judge of his creatures. His own honour is concerned in punishing the guilty. Although everlasting punishment is far worse than annihilation, you have no reason to complain of injustice. Can you estimate the degree of guilt that results from innumerable acts of rebellion against God's authority, majesty and perfection? Only one such act of rebellion renders the sinner guilty. Only the omniscient God knows the true seriousness of sin. Such is its heinousness that the punishment perfectly fits the crime. Think about these solemn truths and may the Lord help you to flee from the wrath to come!

To the believer

Perhaps you profess to believe and embrace this divine truth. You have tasted that the Lord is gracious and you are a real Christian. This doctrine of election tells you where all of your blessings come from and to whom you should give all the glory. You learn that grace is an absolute sovereign who bestows her favours on whoever she pleases without being subject to anyone else. Grace is seen to maintain her rights and assert her honours with a splendour that becomes her. This doctrine sets before you *grace upon the throne* and, like a herald, cries in your ears, 'Bow the knee!'

Election not only teaches you that grace is sovereign, but shows you that, as an object of eternal love, you are completely secure. As Paul says: 'Who shall bring a charge against God's elect?' (Rom. 8:33). It is, therefore, important for you to know that you are one of God's elect and, indeed, such knowledge is attainable. Consider the exhortation of the Holy Spirit through Peter: 'Therefore, brethren, be even more diligent to make your call and election sure...' (2 Peter 1:10); that is, sure to your own mind and conscience. This assurance, when it is based upon truth, is intimately connected with a Christian's peace and joy. Whoever believes that God has called them by the gospel and turned them to Christ can also believe that they have been elected by God. Only God's elect ever experience the new birth and believe in Jesus. If you have embraced this doctrine, you should not only consider it as an article of your faith but also as a doctrine that leads to godliness. Election may be a part of your theological system but it will do you no good unless it produces humility, love, comfort and joy in your life. As it is so connected to experimental religion, you should meditate on it and, considering its importance, seek to defend it from the malicious accusations of those who are proud in their hearts.

If you are, on the authority of Scripture, convinced of the truth of this doctrine and of your own personal election, then remember the glorious privileges to which you have been chosen. You are chosen to share in all the vast gifts of God's grace, culminating in glory with all its eternal happiness. Regeneration, justification, adoption, sanctification and per-severance in faith, not to mention the enjoyment of God himself, are the blessings designed for you in the decree of election. Surely with such blessings in your hands and with such hopes for the future, it is but reasonable that you should be com-pletely devoted to God in seeking to serve and obey him. Grati-tude should invigorate you and love should constrain you in such service. From now on, the glory of God and the honour of

Christ, through whom you enjoy these blessings, should be your main concern and motive in all that you do. Remember how you are described in exalted terms in the holy writings.

Perhaps the most wonderful name that is used of the people of God is 'the elect'. The Spirit of wisdom reminds believers of this name when he urges upon them the responsibilities to which they have been called. He says: 'You are a chosen generation … his own special people' (1 Peter 2:9). The reason for their election as God's special people, as distinguished from others, is stated in the same verse: 'that you may proclaim the praises of him who called you out of darkness into his marvellous light'. This is a Christian's duty, which he should at all times seek to carry out because he was chosen in Christ, that he might be holy and without blame before God in love (Eph. 1:4).

Perhaps you are someone who has a reputation for holding to these sublime truths. Your favourite subjects are God's eternal purposes, absolute sovereignty, unchangeable love and distinguishing grace and yet, you neglect the clearest precepts and most important duties of God's Word. Your life is characterized by pride, covetousness, anger, malice and all kinds of other unholy passions, which make you a scandal to Christianity and cause the godly to be sorrowful. What a grievous condition to be in! You may argue with others in seeking to vindicate divine sovereignty but it will do no good, either to others or yourself. It is clear that you are an enemy in your heart and a rebel in your life against the sovereign God whose rights you claim to uphold. By neglecting his precepts and transgressing his laws, you virtually deny his absolute authority and renounce his supreme dominion. You obey the law of your own sinful lusts and pursue worldly pleasure. You do not love your Maker and Lord, neither do you serve him. May that omnipotent, sovereign grace, which you talk about without experiencing it, deliver and save your soul. Truly, it would be hard to find a more disgusting character outside of hell than you.

The reign of grace

Chapter 4

The reign of grace in our effectual calling

'If you know by experience what it is to be called by grace, then you are happy indeed.'

4.

The reign of grace in our effectual calling

In the previous chapter we saw that grace presided in God's eternal counsels and reigned as an absolute sovereign in the decree of election. We will now consider the same glorious grace in the way it influences the regeneration and *effectual calling* of all who shall ever be saved.

Election does not change the spiritual condition of those God chooses. In election, God considered them as sinful and dying and they continue in this condition until the energy of the Holy Spirit and the power of the gospel reaches their hearts. As God has decreed the means as well as the end to bring about the salvation of the elect, it is absolutely certain that those whom he has chosen in their different generations will be born of the Spirit, converted to Jesus, called by God and have his image renewed within them.

This important change that takes place in the heart and life of a sinner when converted to Christ is often described in God's infallible word as being *called by God, called by grace,* or *called by the gospel.* The eternal Spirit works in conjunction with the gospel in this work of heavenly mercy. All people, in their natural state, are asleep in sin and dead to God, and when they are called, their minds are enlightened and they are given spiritual life. The Spirit of God speaks to the conscience through the truth, quickens the dead sinner, reveals to him his danger and causes him to be afraid. As the Scriptures state: 'The dead will hear the voice of the Son of God; and those who hear will live' (John 5:25). 'Awake you who sleep, arise from the dead, and Christ will give you light' (Eph. 5:14). Sinners have departed from God, are far from him on a road that leads to destruction and are afraid to go back to him. The message of the gospel is: 'Let the wicked ... return to the LORD and he will have mercy on him; and to our God, for he will abundantly pardon' (Isa. 55:7). 'Jesus said to them ... the one who comes to me I will by no means cast out' (John 6:35-37). The Spirit of truth uses these gracious invitations to encourage sinners to return to God and enables them to look for salvation from the God against whom they have sinned and from whom they have turned in their wickedness. This is the character of the heavenly blessing that is the subject of this chapter.

The work of divine grace

If any sinner is called out of darkness and into God's marvellous light, it is only because of divine grace. As the apostle Paul says: 'God called me through his grace' (Gal. 1:15). The saints ascribe their conversion to no other cause than this. Men and women often consider their offences against God as sad failings rather than shocking crimes. Being dead in sin, they do not realize just how evil sin really is, and they foolishly and proudly imagine that their works are good in God's sight. Such people play down their faults and magnify the good that they do. They undervalue the work of Christ and rely on their own so-called fine efforts. They are ignorant of their moral weakness, the total corruption of their hearts and the comprehensive demands of God's law. If they are at all concerned about their souls, they seek to establish their own righteousness as the basis of their acceptance with the high and holy God. They trust in some vague idea of mercy, which comes somehow through Jesus Christ and makes up the deficiencies in their own good works. If they fall into some open and serious sin, they think that if they but forsake it, feel sorry for it and try harder in the future, then out of his love for them God will pardon their sin. Such people imagine that this is the obvious and easy way of obtaining God's favour and forgiveness. So many build their hopes upon this foundation of sand. Therefore, unless reigning grace operates within our hearts to rescue us, we all lie asleep in sin, dreaming of happiness, yet on the edge of a dreadful precipice, unaware of our danger.

Conviction of sin by the Spirit

When the Spirit of God convicts of sin through God's holy law by revealing all of its demands to the conscience of the sinner and the curse to which he is subjected, the sinner begins to feel afraid and often starts to try harder to live a good life. He is aroused from his spiritual slumber and becomes more earnest in religious duties, trying to be holy and seeking after eternal happiness. He no longer performs his acts of devotion to God in a careless and superficial way, which before kept his conscience quiet and gratified his pride. Now, guilt burdens his soul, he experiences sharp pangs of conscience and the terrors of the Almighty seem to be arrayed against him. All the duties that he has neglected, the mercies he has abused and the daring acts of rebellion he has committed against his divine Sovereign crowd in upon his mind and fill his soul with pain. The justice of the Lawgiver appears ready to vindicate the law as holy and good and, like an opponent enflamed with anger, unsheathes the sword against him and loudly demands vengeance. He seeks earnestly to be saved but still, in his pride, he believes that he can achieve salvation by his own efforts. When the Spirit and word of truth reveal to him more of his natural depravity, that his best efforts are defective, that the eternal Judge can only accept a perfect righteousness, his hopes of securing his own salvation vanish and his apprehensions of eternal punishment increase. When the law comes, shining in its purity and operating on the conscience with power, an awareness of his sin is revived, a sense of the deserved wrath of God possesses the soul and all self-righteous hopes come to an end.

He now reflects on his past ignorance and pride with the greatest perplexity and deepest self-abhorrence. Reluctantly, he gives up all ideas about his own moral excellence and is compelled to regard himself as a spiritual leper — unclean! He now realizes that the Scriptures are right to describe the state of the natural man as a filthy sow wallowing in the mud, as a dog in love with its own vomit and as an open tomb sending forth the horrible stench of decaying corpses. He realizes that these things are infinitely less offensive to people than his own moral pollution in the sight of a holy God. What he once saw as trivial sins, he now regards as shocking crimes. He sees that all of the transgressions committed in his life are streams which come from the corrupt fountain within; they proceed from a heart that is desperately wicked. He is astonished and confounded when he reflects upon his inward corruption and depravity.

Now that his eyes have been opened to see the spirituality and vast extent of the divine law, he considers his life to be but one continual act of iniquity. Instead of living every moment of his time in continual and fervent love to God, as required by the law, he sees, to his grief and shame, that he has lived in the love of self and sin. Self-love has been his law and self-pleasing his end. He views the law as a reflection of God's holiness and realizes that he is just as obliged to love God with all the powers of his soul, as he is to not commit the awful crimes of murder and adultery. He considers himself as the 'chief of sinners'.

The awakened sinner understands that drowning his convictions in worldly amusement and pleasure would be useless.

He knows he cannot plead that he is less wicked than others. He realizes that his very prayers and other religious acts are sinful and in need of God's forgiveness. He knows that any future acts of obedience, even if he could perform them perfectly, would not cancel out past sins. He freely and honestly acknowledges his sins to God. He confesses his rebellion and idolatry, the vile lusts of his heart, his irreverence and profanity. He regards the sentence of God's law as just, and though he dreads it, he does not consider it nor the God who gave it as severe, even though he may never experience God's mercy. He says, 'The law is just and I deserve to die.' He wonders if there is a way to be saved that is in harmony with God's holiness, truth and justice.

Conversion to Jesus

He then hears the glorious gospel that tells him that God is not only a just Judge, but also a compassionate Saviour, who has sent his only Son to suffer the wrath of God in the place of sinners. It shows him that there is free forgiveness through faith in the blood of Jesus. The awakened sinner flees to Christ for refuge, knowing that if he is rejected then he must suffer the punishment that he deserves; but if he is accepted, he will be saved and, as a result, God's boundless grace will receive all the glory. So we find that the name and work of Jesus forbid despair and cast a beam of hope upon the soul in darkness.[1]

One would have thought that the gospel of reigning grace, those glad tidings of a Saviour and full salvation offered freely, would be embraced immediately by a sinner so convicted. We would imagine that somebody in this condition would, as soon as he heard the gospel, cry out with joy, 'This is the Saviour I want! This salvation is complete and offered freely to unworthy sinners like me! What amazing grace! This is all that I could

possibly desire! This meets all my needs! In this salvation I will
rest and in this salvation I will glory!'

Sadly, this is not always the case. From observing others
and from one's own experience, it is often the case that the
awakened sinner is reluctant, sometimes extremely reluctant,
to receive comfort from this glorious gospel. This is not because of any defect in the gospel of grace. God's grace is well
able to meet all the needs of the sinner. This reluctance to embrace the Saviour arises from a misunderstanding of grace itself.
He looks for the warrant to receive Christ in himself. He fears
that he has not yet been humbled enough under a sense of sin.
He wonders whether his abhorrence of sin is deep enough. He
is concerned that his desires for Christ and holiness are not as
strong as they should be.[2] Thus sinners can oppose the true
grace of God even when they are under conviction and desire
to be saved. This shows how hard it is for proud sinners to
come to Christ on the basis of grace alone. Indeed, a genuine
self-denial required by the gospel is the hardest sacrifice to
human pride.

The all-sufficiency of Christ

In spite of this reluctance to receive the Saviour in this way,
grace still reigns. It is the Spirit's work in the plan of salvation to
testify of Christ and of sovereign mercy by him and he still
continues to call the awakened and fearful sinner through the
gospel. The Spirit shows to him the all-sufficiency and absolute
freeness of the glorious Redeemer. He convinces him that
those good qualities and righteous acts are not necessary in
coming to the Saviour. Even conviction of sin and a sense
of need should not be considered as conditions of our acceptance and salvation, even though without such conviction and
sense of need nobody would come to Christ to be saved. These
things are necessary, not to incline God to give salvation, but to

incline us to receive it. A sinner will not seek or accept the
wonderful atonement until he becomes aware that he deserves
God's wrath as manifested in hell; and that this is what he
would certainly suffer apart from the propitiation of the lovely
Jesus.

He accepts sinners as they are

I take it for granted that we must come to Christ in the condition in which he calls us. It is clear that he invites us by the
name of sinners. Therefore, we must come to him for life and
salvation as miserable and ruined sinners. The gospel of peace
is preached to and calls such as these. Never forget that the
gospel with all its blessings and Christ with all his fulness are a
glorious provision of God's sovereign grace for the guilty and
wretched; for those who have nothing and can do nothing upon
which to rely. The work of Jesus Christ is intended for those
who are ungodly, pitiful and without hope in themselves. This
was the gracious purpose of God and this is the lovely character
of the gospel. How wonderful this gospel is! It is enough to
make the most depressed person happy. The blessings of grace
were never designed to mark out those who are worthy or
to reward merit, but to help the wretched and save the
desperate.

Rejoice, in that these are the ones who are entitled to heavenly blessings. They have an exclusive right to them. Christ has
nothing to do with, and the gospel has nothing to say to, those
who think that they are better than others, dependent on their
works and unwilling to stand on the same level as tax-collectors
and prostitutes. As they are too proud to live on gospel 'alms'
and to depend on grace entirely for salvation, they must not be
offended if they receive no help at all from grace. In looking to
the law and their good works for salvation, by *these* must they
stand or fall.

He justifies us

Therefore, he who believes in Christ relies on him as the one
who 'justifies the ungodly' (Rom. 4:5). In believing in Christ for
the first time, the sinner regards himself in no other way than
'ungodly'. Otherwise, as Paul indicates, God would not justify
him. The only encouragement that a sinner has to look to Christ
is reigning grace, as it is proclaimed in the gospel. It is not any
inward pious feelings, it is not carrying out certain conditions, it
is not being in any way different to what he was before. The
free declarations of the gospel concerning Jesus contain sufficient
warrant for the vilest sinner, in the most desperate circumstances,
to look for help from the hand of Christ. This is the clear teaching of Scripture: 'I did not come to call the righteous, but sinners,
to repentance' (Mark 2:17). 'For the Son of Man has come to
seek and to save that which was lost' (Luke 19:10). 'Look to
me, and be saved, all you ends of the earth!' (Isa. 45:22). 'Come
to me, all you who labour and are heavy laden, and I will give
you rest' (Matt. 11:28). 'The one who comes to me I will by no
means cast out' (John 6:37). 'Whoever believes in him should
not perish but have everlasting life' (John 3:16).

His work is complete

In these and many other passages of the Scriptures, the sinner
is encouraged to look to the Lord Redeemer with the assurance that if he does, he shall not be disappointed; to look to
him, not as being any different from other people, but as being
guilty and ready to perish. These free declarations are based
on the glorious finished work of Christ who suffered for the
unjust, died for others while they were sinners and ungodly,
and reconciled them to God when they were enemies (1 Peter
3:18; Rom. 5:6-10). All things are now ready for the sinner's
enjoyment and happiness — in this world, a life of faith and

holiness; in the next, the pleasures of glory. The above passages from God's Word are but a few examples of many others that could be mentioned and together, all of them show us the proper ground of our faith in Christ for everlasting salvation.

He alone can save

The sinner who is effectually called by God is not led by the Holy Spirit to believe in a dying Redeemer because he is persuaded that he is now better than his ungodly neighbours and former self. God's Spirit does not bear witness to our spirits concerning our inherent qualities or to tell us that we are better than others. His ministry is to witness to the all-sufficiency, suitability and absolute freeness of Christ, along with all the other blessings that are found only in him. The basis of a believer's hope and the source of his spiritual joy is not that he has done something towards his own salvation (whether believing or anything else) but the truth he believes and the Saviour on whom he relies. This truth, when it is possessed in the heart, becomes the source of his holiness.

As the sinner is brought under the influence of the Spirit and the gospel, he renounces every false hope of being saved by obedience to the law, regards with contempt his own efforts in finding acceptance with God but instead leans on Christ as the Rock of Ages. He clings to the Saviour as the only hope of the guilty and rejoices in him as 'able to save to the uttermost' all those, without exception, 'who come to God through him' (Heb. 7:25). He now sees things that he had not seen before. He beholds with wonder how God can remain just and yet be the justifier of the ungodly, how he can be a just God *and* Saviour at the same time (Rom. 3:26; Isa. 45:21). Now the everlasting covenant unveils its infinite stores to his enraptured sight and the gospel pours its healing balm into his wounded conscience. Jesus Christ and his righteousness are now his only hope. He finds a sufficiency in the glorious Immanuel, not only to supply all of his needs, but to make him infinitely rich and eternally happy. In Christ he rests completely satisfied. A little while before, he stood trembling and confounded at the tribunal of conscience and believed that God must punish him if he were to remain a righteous God. Now he views the work of Christ, the heavenly Substitute, as a full vindication of the rights of justice and an everlasting foundation for his strongest confidence. He finds the gospel to be so suitable, so appropriate to glorify God and yet save the sinner. With astonishment and great joy he beholds *grace on the throne* and he bows and adores. Gratitude abounds in his heart and praise flows from his lips.

Called by God

As he reflects upon his unworthiness, the enmity that he formerly cherished in his heart against his Maker, the carnality of his affections, the stubbornness of his will and his inward pride, he is amazed that he was not cast into hell long ago. He is filled with astonishment as he considers his former reluctance to acknowledge God's sovereignty, his refusal to yield to grace, his resistance to the calls of providence, his stifling of conscience and the fact that if the mighty Spirit had not subdued him, he would have been finally hardened and eternally miserable. As he compares what his offences deserved to what God has bestowed, he cannot but give voice to such amazing mercy. He is convinced from his own experience that his calling must be ascribed to reigning grace. He is fully persuaded that God was the first mover in this, as well as in every other blessing that he has given or will ever give. When he meditates upon his calling, he says, 'I have been found by him, whom I neither loved or sought. The God whom I did not seek has revealed himself to me' (cf. Luke 15:4-5; Rom. 10:20). He says, 'I am known by

God and I am apprehended by Christ', rather than 'I know God and I have apprehended Christ' (cf. Gal. 4:9; Phil. 3:12).

To be called by God in this way is an example of reigning grace and an evidence of electing love. If you know by experience what it is to be called by grace, then you are happy indeed. If these things are true of you, it means that your duty is to walk worthy of your calling, for it is high, holy and heavenly (Eph. 4:1). Your calling is truly noble. You are called out of darkness into marvellous light. You have been called out of a worse bondage than that of Egypt, into the glorious liberty of the sons of God. You are called out of the world, into fellowship with Jesus Christ. You are called out of a state of open rebellion against God and deep distress of soul, into a state of reconciliation and friendship, of conscious peace and heavenly joy. You are called from the slavery of sin, to the practice of holiness. You are called into a state of grace here, and to the enjoyment of glory hereafter. It is the High God who has called you to walk in the way of holiness and to enjoy an unfading inheritance and eternal kingdom. This is both your blessedness and your duty. To consider these things as an incentive to obedience should fire your mind with godly zeal, fill your heart with Christian gratitude, direct your feet in the paths of duty and manifest their constraining influence in all of your conduct.

A warning to the unbeliever

If you are as yet uncalled, then you are in a terrible condition. If you were to leave this world uncalled, then you would be lost for ever and suffer eternal death. Only those who are called here shall be glorified hereafter. If you were to die before being converted to Christ, what would become of you? As dry stubble you would fall into the hands of the one who is a 'consuming fire' (Heb. 12:29). You might be somebody who completely

neglects the concerns of your soul; you might be somebody
who merely dabbles in religious things; you might be somebody who hears the gospel but with careless indifference. Whatever the case may be, if you are not rescued by grace, then the
outcome will be dreadful for you. The word of God and the
gospel of Christ will be a swift witness against you on another
day. The gospel will be 'the aroma of death to death' to your
soul and God himself will be your eternal enemy (2 Cor. 2:16).
'Now consider this, you who forget God, lest I tear you in pieces
and there be none to deliver' (Ps. 50:22).

If you regularly hear the gospel preached and attend the
house of God, do not assume that you are a Christian simply
because you make an open profession of faith and yield a cool
assent to the truth. Thousands have done the same and yet
have perished for ever. If you are not divorced from the law
and renewed in your mind in order to believe in Christ, it will
soon appear that you have chosen a more decent, though less
popular, path to the regions of darkness. You will be damned
with the single advantage of having left a respectable character
among your fellow-sinners. What a pitiful reward for the loss of
your undying soul! What a dreadful end to a religious profession! May God grant that these things are not true of you.

Neither let anyone mistake a profession of evangelical doctrine, whether received by education or picked up from a gospel ministry, for true conversion and faith in the great Redeemer.
A mistake here is fatal and has been the ruin of thousands.
Somebody may have a thorough grasp of doctrine and may
well be able to vindicate the truth against its opposers but his
heart is completely carnal, cold as ice and as barren as a rock.
'Though I ... understand all mysteries and all knowledge ... but
have not love, I am nothing' (1 Cor. 13:2). Empty are the claims
of those, whatever knowledge they have of the gospel, who
live in sin, who do not love God or their neighbour and who
have no desire for God's glory. They may impress with their

religious conversation, they may display their gifts and feed their conceit by defending truth and refuting error. They may, conscious of their superior abilities, look down in pride on people of lesser understanding in the doctrines of grace. But their superior knowledge will only increase their future woe and make their condemnation all the more dreadful.

Notes

1. Do not think that the process of conviction described here is set forth as the standard for all those coming to Christ. I would not limit the Holy One of Israel to the same way of working in the minds of sinners, when he brings them to know themselves, their state and their danger. God is sovereign and acts as he pleases in this, as in everything else. Every sinner must feel his need before he will either seek or accept help at the hand of grace, yet the Lord has various ways to make his people willing in the day of his power. He enlightens some in a more gradual way and draws them to Christ gently and, as it were, with the cords of love. He strikes others with sudden conviction, as with a voice of thunder and a flash of lightening. They are brought to the very brink of despair and shook, as it were, over the bottomless pit. It is not our place to inquire into the reasons for this difference in God's ways. As the Lord saves whom he will, so he may bring them to the knowledge of his salvation in whatever way and by whatever means he pleases. For anyone who is in any doubt as to whether his convictions of sin were genuine, the questions to ask are not: 'How long was I convicted for? Was my sense of sin deep enough? Did I come under conviction through the right means?' Instead the correct questions to answer are: 'Can I honestly say that I know that I have sinned and deserve to perish? Do I believe that nothing but the grace of God can save me? Am I trusting in Jesus Christ alone?'

2. Here it should be well observed that deep distress, arising from the fear of hell, is not required of any, in order to have peace with God. Such distress does not belong to the precepts of the law, but to its curse. Terrifying apprehensions of eternal punishment are not a part of what is required of sinners but what is inflicted on them. There is indeed an evangelical sorrow for sin, which is our duty. This is commanded and has promises attached to it. Legal fears proceed from the curse of the law and not its precept. These express a sense of danger from the law, rather than having done evil against the law. They are certainly not signs of any love to God or of inward holiness. An awakened sinner who desires to know such distress before he can believe is a person seeking the misery of unbelief, that he might obtain a warrant to believe.

The reign of grace

Chapter 5

The reign of grace in the pardon of our sins

'The dreadful penalty due to countless multitudes of the most serious sins is cancelled out, and all because of God's wonderful grace.'

5.
The reign of grace in the pardon of our sins

The pardon of sin is a blessing of tremendous worth because it is absolutely necessary if we are to enjoy a present peace and a future glory. Without it, not one of Adam's race can be happy. When the conscience of a sinner is wounded with guilt and oppressed with fears of God's wrath, this blessing is eagerly desired and sought, and is received joyfully as the first of all favours.

However great this blessing is, were it not for the revelation contained in the Bible, we would be uncertain as to whether there is forgiveness with God. Without the Scriptures, it may well have been suggested that God would not condemn his offending creatures in the end. This, however, would be mere conjecture. God has revealed himself in ways other than the Bible and has made it clear that he is a perfect being who is opposed to all moral evil. However, these other ways are not able to assure us that God forgives sins in a way that is consistent with his own holy character. We are then obliged to adore the condescension and goodness of God, who has not left us groping in the dark to form a thousand wild conjectures about something of such vast importance! When we possess God's precious Word, we are taught with absolute certainty that there is forgiveness with our Maker and Sovereign. This revelation of mercy goes back a long way and was actually known almost from the beginning of time. It was known to the patriarchs but was revealed more clearly in the Mosaic covenant. With the coming of the Son of God, it has received the highest confirmation and shines with the greatest glory. Jehovah's pardoning goodness was proclaimed loudly to Moses and plays an important part in the sacred name by which the God of Israel was known to the church in the wilderness: 'Now the LORD descended in the cloud and stood with him there, and proclaimed the name of the LORD. And the LORD passed before him and proclaimed, "The LORD, the LORD God, merciful and gracious, longsuffering, and abounding in goodness and truth, keeping mercy for thousands, *forgiving iniquity and transgression and sin...* "' (Exod. 34:5-7). To the eternal Sovereign 'belong mercy and forgiveness, though we have rebelled against him' (Dan. 9:9).

This wonderful blessing of the new covenant is represented in the book of God by many powerful metaphors and in a rich variety of language, in order to describe different aspects of sin and its forgiveness. For example, the sinner is described as being defiled with a horrible impurity and his pardon is denoted by the perfect cleansing of his person and by the covering of all his filth (Ps. 14:3; 32:1; 85:2; 1 John 1:7; Rev. 1:5). The sinner is compared to a man who is deep in debt and not able to pay. His pardon is described as a blotting out of the debt, or as not being accounted to him (Ps. 32:2; 51:1, 9; Matt. 18:24). He is likened to a person who is weighed down with a heavy burden on his shoulders. Forgiveness is represented by lifting up and removing the painful load (Ps. 38:4; 32:1; Matt. 11:28). If sin is represented by a black cloud ready to burst in a storm, then forgiveness is said to be a blotting out of that cloud from the face of heaven (Isa. 44:22). Disobedience to God's law is pronounced as rebellion against the Majesty of heaven and the sinner is regarded as a convict under the sentence of death. Forgiveness consists in reversing that sentence and revoking the penalty due. This is the primary way in which God views our sin and pardon and in his grace he says, 'Deliver him from going down to the Pit; I have found a ransom' (Job 33:24). The Lord is also pleased to describe this priceless blessing as casting our sins behind his back; casting them into the depths of the sea; removing them from us as far as the east is from the west; remembering them no more; making our sins which are scarlet and crimson as white as snow and wool (Isa. 38:17; Micah 7:19; Ps. 103:12; Isa. 43:25; Isa. 1:18).

Grace reigns in this forgiveness, in which she displays her riches. The pardon is absolutely perfect. In order for this to be so, three things are required: it must be *full, free* and *everlasting*. That is, forgiveness must extend to all sin; it must be given without the sinner having to meet any conditions; it must be absolutely irreversible. Let us consider these three things in more detail.

Full forgiveness

This forgiveness must be full. It must include all sins, however many there are, however serious they are. Sin is a transgression of God's law and every single transgression is enough to subject the offender to a dreadful curse. Therefore, if the guilt of *every* sin is not removed and the penalty revoked, the curse must fall on us and God's wrath must be our portion. Full pardon is essential in order for us to be happy and so it is granted to sinners. The Scriptures declare that when the offended sovereign God pardons anyone, he forgives all their sins. The Lord of hosts says, 'I will cleanse them from all their iniquity by which they have sinned against me, and I will pardon all their iniquities by which they have sinned and by which they have transgressed against me' (Jer. 33:8). What a lovely declaration of grace! It is God's prerogative to forgive sin and this he declares he will do. When he does forgive, he does not forgive some sins only, but all.

Notice the words of another ambassador from the court of heaven. With thanksgiving and joy, the prophet Micah declares of the eternal King: 'He will again have compassion on us, and will subdue our iniquities. You will cast all our sins into the depths of the sea' (Micah 7:19). Here we learn that God is so gracious and kind in removing, not just some sins, but all sins. He will cast them out of his sight for ever. Another writer of God's infallible word expresses this glorious truth with similar delight: 'Bless the LORD, O my soul; and all that is within me, bless his holy name! ... Who forgives all your iniquities, who heals all your diseases' (Ps. 103:1, 3). What a firm foundation for continual thanksgiving! Whenever God forgives sin, he forgives it so completely that he 'has not observed iniquity', which 'shall not be found' (Num. 23:21; Jer. 50:20; Rom. 8:33). Therefore there is no condemnation for those who receive God's forgiveness.

For the worst of sinners

This forgiveness is worthy of God and wholly meets the needs of the worst of sinners. It proceeds from sovereign grace and reaches the foulest crimes and most abhorrent transgressions. By this gracious pardon, scarlet and crimson sins are made as white as wool and even whiter than the snow. This is seen in the life of Manasseh who shed much innocent blood in Jerusalem yet was forgiven. In his bitter anger Saul of Tarsus persecuted the church but was pardoned. The thief on the cross had led a life of sin and crime and even taunted the Son of God. He too was forgiven in his dying moments. These heinous sins, and even worse, have been pardoned by a gracious God. This is because the blood of Christ, who was the incarnate Son of God when he died, has infinite power. His blood is able to cleanse from all sin (1 John 1:7). The dreadful penalty due to countless multitudes of the most serious sins is cancelled out and all because of God's wonderful grace.

There is hope

If the worst of sinners only knew what forgiveness there is with God, they would no longer believe the fatal lie of the devil, that there is no hope. Jehovah is a God of pardon. This is his name and glory. The Lord says, 'I will pardon all their iniquities … then it shall be to me a name of joy, a praise, and an honour before all nations of the earth, who shall hear all the good that I do to them' (Jer. 33:8-9). What amazing words! The Sovereign of all worlds seems to glory in pardoning mercy, as one of the brightest jewels in his own eternal crown. No wonder the church cries out with such abundant joy, 'Who is a God like you, pardoning iniquity and passing over the transgression of the remnant of his heritage? He does not retain his anger for ever, because he delights in mercy' (Micah 7:18).

There is help

Do you tremble at the number and seriousness of your sins? Then consider the riches of God's grace. Though by nature you are a child of wrath, though you have violated the law of God and have incurred its everlasting curse, though you are a rebel against a sovereign God, though your sins of every kind call out for vengeance to fall on your guilty head, though the devil accuses you and tempts you to despair, there is still help at hand. Despite all of these things, there is no reason to sink without hope. Look! There is full forgiveness with God and such is his mercy that he waits, ready to graciously bestow these precious blessings (Isa. 30:18). God never withholds his forgiveness because certain sins are particularly heinous. To dispute this is to deny that salvation is by grace. His mercy is not conditional, narrow or limited. Unlike men, God never waits to see something good in others before he will show mercy. It is sovereign and absolutely free.

Remember that multitudes now inhabit heaven, that place of purity and joy, who were once guilty sinners. They once were fearful and ready to be overcome with despair. They were as sinful and pitiful as you are, if not worse. In heaven dwell the 'spirits of just men made perfect' and yet once, before God had mercy on them, they were no better than you (Heb. 12:23). You will find in heaven the idolatrous and murderous Manasseh (2 Kings 21; 2 Chron. 33). You will see the faithless Peter, the man who, despite the warnings of his Master, denied his Lord and Saviour with oaths and curses (Mark 14:71). There you will see many of the shameless Corinthians, people who were once a reproach to their nation and a scandal to humanity. Near to the very Son of God, seated on thrones of bliss, you will behold many sinners from Jerusalem who were guilty of the blood of our Lord. The sight of these among the shining hosts must surely encourage the despairing sinner. Though your debt is enormous and your sins innumerable, yet God's forgiveness is full and is well able to meet your need. Rest and rejoice in this.

Free forgiveness

The next essential requirement in a complete pardon is that it is free. This means that there must not be any conditions for the sinner to meet in order to be forgiven. In fact, it was Christ, our Surety, who did everything so that we might be forgiven. Our pardon depended upon him fulfilling the conditions and terms laid down by his Father. These were both hard and dreadful in that the Son of God had to become man, obey God's law perfectly and then suffer the humiliating death of the cross. The strict condition and dreadful demand laid upon Christ as our substitute was the shedding of his own blood. This was the righteous requirement of God's justice. 'Without shedding of blood there is no remission' (Heb. 9:22). This was true, even for the Prince of life and Lord of glory. The atonement of our glorious High Priest satisfies the claims of God's justice, obtains the pardon of sin and brings peace to the consciences of those who are distressed with a sense of guilt.

With divine mercy

This forgiveness is absolutely free to the pardoned sinner. It is bestowed according to the riches of divine mercy and is received according to grace. As it is written: 'In him we have redemption through his blood, the forgiveness of sins, according to the riches of his grace' (Eph. 1:7). Christ's death is the cause, and God's glory is the ultimate reason why he bestows this blessing, as the Scriptures teach: 'God in Christ forgave you' (Eph. 4:32); 'I, even I, am he who blots out your transgressions for my own sake' (Isa. 43:25).

In the preceding verses to this last reference, serious charges are brought by God against his sinful people. We would have thought that the Lord would proclaim their utter destruction. Instead, he assures them that he will blot out their transgressions, not because of anything in them, but to demonstrate the riches of his grace and display his glory. Here we find an example of Paul's declaration: 'Where sin abounded, grace abounded much more' (Rom. 5:20). Israel were highly favoured by the Lord and yet they neglected their duty to him. They had stopped seeking their God in prayer and found his worship to be wearisome. They had burdened God with their sins and wearied him by their iniquities, and yet they are pardoned! What amazing mercy! Sin abounds like a flood but grace abounds like an ocean. If words mean anything, all of this shows that forgiveness is absolutely free.

With kindness

In another place the Lord says, again through the prophet Isaiah, 'For the iniquity of his covetousness I was angry and struck him; I hid and was angry, and he went on backsliding in the way of his heart' (Isa. 57:17). What does the Lord try next? These milder methods had failed to turn the sinner back to himself. It might be expected that he would lay severer strokes upon him and make him feel the vengeance of his raised arm. Surely he will teach him not to offend any more by inflicting an awful punishment upon him. This is what men would do in dealing with someone who stubbornly refuses correction. However, reigning grace does wonders, such wonders as will fill heaven with hallelujahs to all eternity. God's way of dealing with his hardened enemies is unlike our own. The Lord continues: 'I have seen his ways, and will heal him; I will also lead him, and restore comforts to him and to his mourners' (Isa. 57:18). Their spiritual diseases are healed, their sins are pardoned, they are led in ways of holiness and made partakers of heavenly comfort and joy! Amazing grace indeed!

Examples from the New Testament

Let us consider some of those everlasting monuments of reigning grace recorded for us in the New Testament. All of these received the free pardon of their sins.

Saul

Saul, who later became Paul, was a cruel persecutor of the children of God. Luke tells us that Saul breathed out 'threats and murder' against the saints of the Most High (Acts 9:1). If it had been in his power, he would have destroyed all the

Christians then living. He was like an animal in human form, pursuing and devouring the innocent lambs of Christ. Later, he testified to his former rage and malice against the peaceful and holy disciples of Jesus: 'I punished them often in every synagogue and compelled them to blaspheme; and being exceedingly enraged against them, I persecuted them even to foreign cities' (Acts 26:11), which revealed how bitterly he hated those whose only offence was that they loved our Lord and acknowledged him to be the true Messiah. This stirred up his anger, so much so, that he did not want them to live. When he came to his right mind, he confessed, 'I was formerly a blasphemer, a persecutor and an insolent man' (1 Tim. 1:13). Yet this very man, this enemy of Christ and murderer of his people, 'obtained mercy'. Suddenly, just when his thoughts were of slaughter and his heart thirsted for blood, just as he was on the way to persecute believers and eradicate the memory of a crucified Messiah from the earth, at that very moment, the Saviour chose to demonstrate his love to him. He was powerfully struck with conviction, called by grace, pardoned and justified and became an heir of eternal salvation. Saul was not required to fulfil any condition, either to entitle him to or qualify him for these blessings. He has told us himself that the grace of our Lord was 'exceedingly abundant' towards him (1 Tim. 1:14). In Saul's life although 'sin abounded, grace abounded much more' (Rom. 5:20).

Someone may think that the grace shown to Paul was as unique and unusual as the manner of his conversion. Paul himself says, 'For this reason I obtained mercy, that in me first Jesus Christ might show all longsuffering, as a *pattern* to those who are going to believe on him for everlasting life' (1 Tim. 1:16). It is clear that the longsuffering and grace manifested in the conversion and pardon of Saul are not to be considered as something rarely repeated but as a very example of the normal way of grace. The way in which he was converted *was* unique and unusual but the grace shown to him was not.

Zacchaeus

Zacchaeus was one of the chief tax collectors and, most probably, one of the chief extortioners. His fellow countrymen regarded his employment as detestable because he was collecting taxes for the hated Romans and was also getting rich by cheating his fellow Jews. Only an apostate son of Abraham would do such things. Those whom he usually invited to his house were sinners of the worst sort. Yet Zacchaeus was converted and forgiven. There were no duties to perform or qualifications to meet prior to his believing and repenting. 'Jesus said to him, "Today salvation has come to this house"' (Luke 19:9). Here is another example of free and unconditional pardon.

The woman of Samaria

The woman of Samaria was ignorant of God and of the true way of worshipping him (John 4). She was living in adultery when our Lord met with her. Jesus made himself known to her and she believed upon him, confessed her faith and received the forgiveness of her sins, without having to fulfil any conditions or perform any duties beforehand.

The Philippian jailer

The conversion of the Philippian jailer is another good example of free forgiveness (Acts 16). This man was a Gentile idolater, a cruel persecutor of God's servants and was about to commit the terrible sin of self-murder. Being awakened in his conscience, he was told by Paul to believe on the Lord Jesus Christ, with the strongest assurance that in so doing he would be saved. There is no intimation that Paul and Silas demanded any conditions to be met before he could believe. They did not require religious duties to be performed or a period of deep humiliation or evidences of love to God before the jailer could believe and be saved. They told him to trust immediately in the Saviour who is freely available to the very worst of sinners. As we believe that Paul and Silas reflected the mind of God in this, we assert that good desires, holiness or the fruit of the Spirit are not required as the condition of pardon.

The dying thief

I could give other examples to show that God's forgiveness is given freely to sinners but I will only give one more — the thief who died at the same time as our Lord.

This man died the most shameful of deaths. Crucifixion was only used for those guilty of the most appalling crimes. This is what he deserved and his own conscience acknowledged it. He was a hardened criminal. Matthew describes him as a robber and tells us that he hurled insults at our dying Lord, along with the crowd (Matt. 27:44). He and his fellow criminal were vile sinners, guilty of blaspheming the Son of God to the utmost of their powers. They must have known that Jesus was being crucified for claiming to be the Christ, the Son of the living God. Yet they reviled and reproached the most glorious person who has ever lived, even when he was dying in such excruciating pain on the cross. They did not show the least sign of repentance for their sins, but showed the deepest hatred towards the bleeding Immanuel; they were hardened concerning God and showed no concern for the things of eternity.

This was the condition of this thief as he was dying. These were the 'qualifications' that he had before he was forgiven. Yet, he was forgiven! Let reigning grace have all the glory! He realized something of who Jesus was and why he was suffering. When his fellow thief continued to revile Jesus, he rebuked him sharply for it. He prayed to the dying Jesus and acknowledged him to be Lord of heaven, having authority to give crowns and thrones to whoever he wishes. In this, he paid Jesus the highest honour that mortals can pay to the true God. His petition was: 'Lord, remember me when you come into your kingdom' (Luke 23:42). Jesus answered him with a majesty and condescension which becomes the Supreme Possessor of heaven and earth: 'Assuredly, I say to you, today you will be with me in paradise' (Luke 23:43). The prayer of this man assumes that his faith was in the Saviour and our Lord's gracious answer proves it. Surely his sins were all forgiven. If not, how could our Saviour assure him of a place in heaven? There is no hint that this ungodly criminal performed any duty or met any conditions, in order to qualify himself to receive salvation.

We would have thought that the prayer, 'Remember me', would only be accepted from the dying lips of prophets, apostles and martyrs; those who had led lives of holiness and faithful service to God. This thief knew that he was only a wicked criminal and yet he uttered these words with such boldness and his prayer was answered. How can we explain this? What could possibly make such a vile sinner so bold? The only answer is the reigning grace of God. This grace is the only basis of hope for the greatest apostles and the most holy Christians in the world, as well as blasphemers, persecutors, thieves and murderers.

Let us behold with wonder the amazing grace of our Lord Redeemer in choosing this man to accompany him to paradise. He had not, like Enoch, walked with God. He had not, like Abraham, longed for the day of Christ, with joy and anticipation. He had not, like Simeon, waited eagerly for the consolation of Israel. He was a man who, to all intents and purposes, had devoted his time and energy to the service of Satan. The sword of civil justice had not permitted him to live and, in the eyes of the people, he was even less worthy of mercy than the notorious murderer Barabbas. How wonderful is the way of Jesus, the Judge of the world! When such a wicked man is saved, who can despair? In the conversion of this man it seems to have been Jehovah's intention to show that the salvation which Jesus was then accomplishing originated in sovereign mercy, flowed in atoning blood, met the needs of the worst sinners and terminated in his own glory as its ultimate purpose.

Sovereignty of grace

What an example we have here of the power of God's grace! At first we see this thief as a hardened criminal. A few hours later we hear him pray to Jesus and express his repentance. Before the day has ended, even whilst his dead body is still hanging on the cross, his immortal soul enters paradise into the very presence of God. As a nuisance to society and a pest to the public he is executed on a cross and from there he is transported to a throne of glory! We also behold here the sovereignty of grace. The other thief was as unworthy of salvation as the one who was saved. Yet, he was unrepentant when he died and was lost for ever. Here the Almighty shows that he will have mercy on whomever he will have mercy (Rom. 9:15).

God's perfect plan

I cannot conclude my comments on the dying thief without stating that the death of the Son of God was intended to give a basis for hope to the very worst sinners and that the circumstances surrounding his death were wisely designed to confirm this. The Prince of life was 'numbered with the transgressors' (Isa. 53:12). He was crucified between two thieves. He died, not only by means of the most horrific form of death, but in the worst possible company.

This did not happen by chance; it was planned by Jehovah and predicted in the Old Testament. It was graciously ordered so that the most wicked sinners might be encouraged to seek the Lord. From this we realize that our Lord's death was not intended for the more respectable part of mankind, who believe that they are good enough already. If this were the case, what hope would there be for notorious criminals and those who consider themselves to be guilty and worthless? There would be nothing but despair for them. Supposing men with a reputation for godliness, such as Noah, Daniel and Job, had been crucified with our Lord, it would still be true that he was numbered with the transgressors. However, this would have provided small encouragement to those who are not only condemned by God's law, but who have, through their actions, incurred public hostility. Such people might have concluded that their situation was completely hopeless and ended their days in despair and in the pursuit of sinful pleasures.

Reigning grace is very unwilling for this to happen and so the Holy One of Israel not only died for sinners, but also died between two criminals. This shows that the best of men have no solid grounds for hope apart from the blood of the cross, and that the worst sinner has no reason to sink in despair, because he sees the Lord of life die between these criminals and even take one of them with him to heaven!

Do not be offended if I assert that you stand on the same level with this thief, in terms of acceptance with God. Indeed, the most upright person living has nothing more to plead before his Maker than he did. Salvation is all of grace and grace is unconditional favour. Therefore, grace pays no regard to any supposed or real differences between men. All are considered as guilty sinners. We conclude that whoever looks for salvation by any other grace than which saved this thief will be terribly disappointed.

The effects of free forgiveness

In these examples of the free pardon of sin, we have seen the majesty and power of grace. These examples have especially been preserved in the inspired Scriptures in order to show us the actions and procedures of the court of heaven. They are intended for our observation, instruction and comfort. They were ordered to be passed down to posterity by the eternal King 'that in the ages to come he might show the exceeding riches of his grace in his kindness towards us in Christ Jesus' (Eph. 2:7).

Changed lives

The effects of free forgiveness in the lives of these wicked sinners is worthy of our notice and testifies to the truth of God's Word: 'There is forgiveness with you, that you may be feared' (Ps. 130:4). When Paul experienced the power and tasted the sweetness of pardoning grace, no labours were too great and no sufferings were too severe, for the sake of his Lord. He did not count his life dear, so that he might spread the glorious gospel and promote his Redeemer's honour. Zacchaeus was changed in a moment, made restitution to those he had cheated and gave generously to the poor. The woman of Samaria immediately invited others to hear that gracious voice which had brought life to her own soul and to receive him as the Christ. The jailer showed a willingness to obey the commands of the King of Zion, by submitting to the ordinance of baptism. He gave evidence of his love of the truth by washing the wounds of Paul and Silas and by giving them hospitality in his home. The thief, in those few moments which he had to live, confessed his offences, acknowledged the justice of his punishment and, out of love to his fellow criminal, reproved him for his blasphemy and warned him of his great danger.

These examples are quite sufficient to prove that forgiveness is free and not dependent on any conditions being fulfilled or works being performed by the sinner. I could mention many other examples and declarations from the Scriptures but I think that one will suffice. The apostle Paul says, 'When we were enemies we were reconciled to God through the death of his Son' (Rom. 5:10). The forgiveness of sin is an important part of our being reconciled to God. The Apostle teaches that this forgiveness and reconciliation occurred when we were God's enemies. This also shows that forgiveness is absolutely free because God is said to forgive his enemies and not his friends.

An understanding of the wisdom of God's grace in salvation

As we reflect that sinners cannot be pardoned without our incarnate God shedding his precious blood, we realize just how serious sin is. When we consider the dignity of the one who suffered for sin and the full weight of the wrath of God which he bore, we affirm that the sufferings of Christ reveal the exceeding sinfulness of sin and the purity of God, far more than the punishment of sinners in hell. We see clearly that our Sovereign is both just and merciful in granting a free pardon to the worthless and guilty. We behold the righteous Judge and the suffering Saviour, inflexible justice and triumphant grace in harmony together. The curse is executed in all its rigour, and mercy is manifested in all its riches. Here the Lord of all is seen, granting free forgiveness to multitudes but in a way that preserves the honour of his law and maintains the rights of his government. Even the angels are amazed at the wisdom and grace of God in these things. Distressed consciences may rest in this method of forgiveness. God's way of saving sinners certainly impresses the mind with a sense of the infinite evil of sin, the holiness of God and the comprehensive demands of his law. However, it also encourages the utmost confidence in the mercy and grace of God which he has revealed.

An understanding of God's supreme wisdom

In the light of the freeness of God's forgiveness, it is shocking to think that there are those who teach that pardon for sin cannot be received until the sinner is prepared for it. This may be through a period of being humbled or of self-denial or of living a holy life. In this way, they distort and hide the true glory of God's grace. This pardon is not in any way conditional upon what we do but flows from sovereign grace and is designed by Jehovah to magnify his grace before the redeemed and the angels, in this world and the next. In forgiving sinners, the Lord shows that he is infinitely superior to all his creatures in their acts of forgiveness. His forgiveness becomes him as God. It is written: 'I will not execute the fierceness of my anger; I will not again destroy Ephraim' (Hosea 11:9). What is the reason given for such forbearance? 'For I am God, and not man.' In the context of his mercy to sinners, God says, 'For my thoughts are not your thoughts, nor are your ways my ways ... For as the heavens are higher than the earth, so are my ways higher than your ways, and my thoughts than your thoughts' (Isa. 55:8-9). He freely forgives our 'ten thousand talents' and we are reluctant to forgive others their 'hundred denarii' (Matt. 18:21-35). So it is that the Lord exceeds all our expectations and thoughts in bestowing a full and free pardon on the guilty. May a sense of this free forgiveness rest on your mind, comfort your heart and stir up your love. This forgiveness is an incentive to fear and love; to adore and obey the Lord; to be 'filled with the fruits of righteousness which are by Jesus Christ, to the glory and praise of God' (Phil. 1:11).

Everlasting forgiveness

I now want to show that God's forgiveness is everlasting and irreversible. This glorious truth is taught in many places within the holy Scriptures; for example, in that lovely clause in the new covenant: 'For I will be merciful to their unrighteousness, and their sins and their lawless deeds I will remember no more' (Heb. 8:12). This declaration enters into the very heart of the new and better and unchangeable covenant. If the Lord, whose royal prerogative it is to punish or pardon, declares that he will remember our sins no more, we may be assured that it is an everlasting pardon and will not be reversed. This declaration is more than a promise. Of course, a promise from God is sure and certain but this promise comes in the form of a covenant. It is an absolute promise, which God, in his faithfulness, is obliged to fulfil. We continue in a state of pardon, not because of our works, but because of the ongoing power of our Lord's atonement and the absolute faithfulness of God to his covenant. Once God grants his forgiveness to us, he will never rescind it. That forgiveness will remain upon us in all its power and glory.

Irreversible

This comforting truth is also taught by David: 'As far as the east is from the west, so far has he removed our transgressions from us' (Ps. 103:12). This implies that the sins of those who are forgiven shall never come against them, unless the two opposite points of east and west should meet, which is impossible. In another place David says, 'Blessed is he whose transgression is forgiven' (Ps. 32:1). This can only be true if the forgiveness is full, free and everlasting. If not, what peace of conscience could we enjoy here and what hope could we have of glory hereafter? God's continual pardon does not depend on our continual obedience. Every time we sin, we do not come under God's wrath and condemnation again. If these things were true, David would hardly describe the forgiven sinner as 'blessed'. If our pardon is not everlasting and irreversible then we are left in a very uncertain condition. In fact, it would be very unlikely that we would ever obtain eternal happiness. With our future hope becoming so precarious, our present peace would be taken away.

No more condemnation

The same truth is expressed in this way: 'You will cast all their sins into the depths of the sea' (Micah 7:19). Transgressions are compared, by the inspired writer, to a stone or some other heavy object, which when cast into the sea, cannot be recovered by men. Anything, even something as huge as a mountain, which is thrown into the vast ocean disappears and is lost for ever. By this striking image, the Holy Spirit teaches that the forgiveness of the believer by God is everlasting. Similarly the Lord says, 'The iniquity of Israel shall be sought, but there shall be none; and the sins of Judah, but they shall not be found; for I will pardon those whom I preserve' (Jer. 50:20). Again, this proves that those who are pardoned by the God of grace have all their sins forgiven for ever. The Lord, speaking through Isaiah to the Jewish church, says, '"For as I have sworn that the waters of Noah would no longer cover the earth, so have I sworn that I would not be angry with you, nor rebuke you. For the mountains shall depart and the hills be removed, but my kindness shall not depart from you, nor shall my covenant of peace be removed," says the Lord, who has mercy on you' (Isa. 54:9-10). Here we have, not only the word of the Lord, but his oath as well, to assure his people of his forgiving mercy.

The apostle Paul challenges and defies every enemy of the believer with these words: 'Who shall bring a charge against God's elect? ... Who is he who condemns?' (Rom. 8:33-34). These bold words would be meaningless if the blessing of forgiveness could be reversed or if the sinner, having been acquitted, could fall again under condemnation.

The forgiveness of sins is an important part of the message of the gospel. The joyful language of this message is: 'Let it be known to you, brethren, that through this man is preached to you the forgiveness of sins' (Acts 13:38). This is the testimony of the gospel and the glorious blessing of pardon is received by faith in the dying Redeemer. As it is written: 'To him all the prophets witness that, through his name, whoever believes in him will receive remission of sins' (Acts 10:43). By believing the infallible record that God has given of his Son, we are reconciled to God. The propitiating blood of Christ is sprinkled on our hearts, pardon is applied to our consciences and peace is enjoyed in our souls.

The constant care of God

The truth of free forgiveness is in no way contrary to the fact that the Lord lays his chastening hand on those he forgives. Believers are corrected because of their backslidings but these chastisements only show that God loves his children and exercises a constant care over them. In this way the believer is assured that the Lord will never take his lovingkindness from him nor allow his faithfulness to fail (Ps. 89:33).

That believers are commanded, in the Scriptures, to pray continually for the forgiveness of their sins, in no way contradicts what I have said about forgiveness being full, free and everlasting. When a believer sins, he does not come under God's condemnation again. He remains a child of God but he needs the application of pardoning grace to his soul, so that his relationship with God might be restored. Every day, believers sin against God, grieve his Spirit and wound their consciences. Every day, they need the fresh sprinklings of the blood of Jesus and a renewed sense of forgiveness and it is their duty to seek these things at the throne of grace.

How glorious is the forgiveness that I have been describing! It is perfect and so suitable to the needs of poor and guilty sinners. Everything about it encourages the most unworthy and guilty person to seek it from the God of mercy. For this pardon to bring peace to our consciences and salvation to our souls, it is essential that it is full, free and everlasting.

Anything less would not meet all our needs. If it is not full forgiveness, we would still have to suffer everlastingly for those sins which are not pardoned. If it is not free forgiveness, we could not possibly meet the required conditions to be pardoned. If it is not everlasting forgiveness, we would be always anxious lest that pardon be reversed because of our sins. Therefore, no one should be discouraged from looking to the Lord for this blessing.

In conclusion

What do you think of this glorious pardon? Does it meet your needs? Is it worthy of your acceptance? Perhaps you are somebody who is careless and at ease in your sins. Perhaps you are eagerly pursuing the pleasures of this uncertain life. Can you be content to live and die without knowing this forgiveness? Do you regard your need of God's pardon as unimportant? Let me remind you that you have sinned, you are condemned and, without forgiveness, you will suffer everlasting death. You are on the edge of an awful precipice. Wake up from your sleep! In the next hour you could be swept into eternity, brought before the Judge of all and be beyond the possibility of help. Another moment and your life could be at an end and you will be lost for ever. May God in his grace not allow you to continue any longer in such a dreadful condition.

Are you aware of your need and longing for forgiveness? Then look to the dying Jesus. It is true that your iniquities abound but pardoning mercy, through his atoning death, abounds much more. Rejoice and be encouraged because the pardon you desire is a free gift. Blessed be God for such amazing mercy!

How wonderful that your eternal salvation and God's glory are bound up in the free bestowal of this forgiveness! Do not stand trembling at a distance! You may seek boldly for pardon from God, through the blood of Christ, and God has declared in his truth that you will not be disappointed.

Do you know already the pardoning goodness of God? Having been forgiven much, you should love much (Luke 7:47). The remembrance of such a rich blessing should enlarge your heart with holy affections towards your Redeemer, stir up your heart to worship and make you zealous in every good work. This high favour should cause you to show compassion to those who offend you. God has forgiven your 'ten thousand talents', you should forgive others their 'hundred denarii' (Matt. 18:21-35). This forgiveness, far from being an incentive to evil, will incline your heart towards that which is good. It will cause you to love God and to abhor all that opposes his holiness and revealed will. A sense of pardon on your mind will produce in you a godly sorrow for sin, whether hidden in your heart or openly manifested in your life, and will cause you to confess it to God with shame and grief. These are the effects of God's forgiveness and these fruits will appear in various degrees in those who know this blessing. However, those who profess to be forgiven but who still live under the dominion of sin and do not forgive others are sadly deluded.

The reign of grace

'Believers are declared by the infallible Spirit to be justified in him; accepted in him; and saved in him. This is the God-appointed method of justification and the provision made by grace for the final acceptance of guilty, ungodly and wretched creatures.'

6.

The reign of grace in our justification

The doctrine of justification plays a prominent role in that religion which is revealed from above and which was once delivered to the saints (Jude 3). This doctrine, far from being a matter of speculation, influences all other aspects of truth and has an important bearing upon all Christian experience and practical godliness. It has such great importance that any misunderstanding over it has many dangerous and far-reaching consequences. This is patently obvious when we consider how justification is concerned with a sinner's acceptance with God. If we do not understand justification, then other gospel truths, with which it is intimately connected, become disjointed. Justification must be viewed as a fundamental article of the faith and requires our serious consideration.

What justification means

How can a sinner be right with God? This is a question of infinite importance to every child of Adam. Such a question could never have been answered by human or angelic reasoning unless the Lord of heaven and earth had not revealed his sovereign grace towards his disobedient and rebellious creatures. God has provided an answer in the gospel. By reading the Scriptures, the youngest believer can know the way to be right with

God. In his good pleasure, God often reveals this glorious truth to those who are despised by proud intellectual people, so that no one might have the least ground for boasting.

Legal justification

Justification is a legal term and signifies *the declaring or pronouncing a person righteous according to law.* Justification does not make a person righteous within. It is the work of sanctification to make a sinner holy. Justification is the work of a judge who pronounces that a person is acquitted from all judicial charges. We can see that this blessing does not consist in an inward change of heart when we realize that the opposite of justification is condemnation. If a man is condemned in court it does not mean that he has been made a criminal by that declaration. Evil is not infused into his mind, neither is he made guilty. It is the function of the court to try the man according to the law and, if he is proved to be guilty, it is the judge's responsibility to declare him guilty and to sentence him to the appropriate punishment. It follows that the person who is justified is declared to be righteous in the eyes of the law, with the right to live. In the Scriptures, justification is called the 'justification of life' (Rom. 5:18). The words justify, justified and justification are used in God's Word in this legal sense and are opposite to the words condemn, condemned and condemnation.

In a theological sense, justification can be either legal or evangelical. If someone could be found who has kept God's law perfectly, he would be justified by his own obedience. This is 'legal justification'. However, nobody can be justified or stand acquitted before God by this means. The Scriptures are clear: 'There is none righteous, no, not one' (Rom. 3:10). The whole world, having transgressed, is guilty before this eternal Judge and is under sentence of death by his righteous law. On this basis, everyone is excluded from hope and abandoned to utter destruction. The law can only accept a perfect righteousness and must punish with eternal death those who fall under its curse.

Evangelical justification

The justification of which the Scriptures speak is not a personal but an imputed righteousness. Only this righteousness can meet the needs of sinners. It is a 'righteousness ... apart from the law' (Rom. 3:21). It is provided by grace and revealed in the gospel and is what is meant by an 'evangelical justification'. In this justification there is a most wonderful display of God's justice and his boundless grace.

It is important to make the distinction between our justification in the sight of God and in the sight of other people. The former is by grace alone, through faith. The latter is by works. We are thinking about the former in this chapter and may define it in the following way: 'Justification is a judicial but gracious act of God, by which a sinner is absolved from the guilt of sin, is freed from condemnation and receives a right to eternal life, only for the sake of Christ's obedience, which is imputed to him and received by faith.'

God's prerogative

It is God's prerogative to justify. The one whom we have offended by numerous acts of rebellion has the sole right to acquit the guilty and pronounce them righteous. Jehovah, whose judgement is always according to truth, justifies all who believe in Jesus. Here grace reigns. In his wisdom God appoints the way, in his mercy he provides the means, and in his grace he imputes righteousness and pronounces the sinner acquitted. He does everything in perfect agreement with the demands of his violated law and the rights of his offended justice.

When we study the Scriptures, we find that all three persons of the Godhead are involved in our justification, each having a distinct part to play. The *Father* is represented as the one who appoints the way in giving his own Son to perform the conditions of our acceptance before him. The *Son* obeyed the law perfectly and made atonement for sin in order to provide the righteousness by which we are justified. The *Holy Spirit* reveals to sinners what Christ has done and enables them to receive his righteousness through faith. The Spirit also testifies of this justification within the conscience of the believer. It is the triune God who justifies. We can then use the triumphant language of Paul: 'Who is he who condemns?' (Rom. 8:34). If Jehovah acquits the sinner, who in earth or hell shall reverse the sentence? There is no higher court to which any appeal can be made. There is no superior tribunal at which a complaint can be lodged against those who have been justified by the eternal God. When he acquits the sinner, he absolves him from all guilt and accepts him as completely righteous. This perfect justification shall never be rendered void, not by the unworthiness of the one who is justified nor by the accusations of Satan. It shall stand firmer than the everlasting hills and be as unshaken as the throne of God. All the other blessings of the eternal covenant, including the happiness of glory itself, flow out from it.

Must be earnestly sought

This blessing is so great and glorious. It is to be earnestly sought and thankfully enjoyed. Can anyone who is conscious of being justified cease to rejoice in his Justifier? Can anyone who is convinced of his guilty and condemned condition cease to pray and long for it? Are you aware of the value of this blessing? Do you desire to be justified? If not, you are still in your sins and under condemnation; this justification is far from you. What if you should never be justified? What if you never know God's forgiveness and acceptance and you die under the curse already passed upon you? How dreadful your condition would be and yet, you would have no reason to complain. You have trampled God's authority under your feet and cherished a spirit of enmity against him. As your conscience testifies, you have not obeyed God's law or loved his gospel. Your main purpose in life has been, not to please God, but to gratify your lusts and carry out your sinful ambitions. You have never seriously considered the death of the Son of God, the greatest event that has ever taken place and the only thing that can save you from final condemnation. Remember that you will be brought into God's court and tried by the Judge of all. An eternal hell or an eternal heaven will be the outcome for you. How can you rest, not knowing whether the Judge will absolve or condemn you? May the God of grace wake you up, so that you begin to ask the question: 'How can a man be righteous before God?' (Job 9:2).

For the ungodly

The Scriptures teach us that God justifies the ungodly. 'Now to him who works, the wages are not counted as grace but as debt. But to him who does not work but believes on him who justifies the ungodly, his faith is accounted for righteousness' (Rom. 4:4-5). From this important text we learn that those whom God justifies, not only are devoid of a perfect righteousness, but also have no good works at all! They have no spiritual qualities and no righteous inclinations. They are considered as ungodly when this blessing is bestowed upon them. In this way grace is exalted and reigns in our justification. The Scriptures teach repeatedly that we are justified by grace, and we have already seen how grace is the complete opposite of works.

For the unworthy

Therefore, whoever is justified by grace is considered as un-worthy at the very moment when this blessing is bestowed. This momentous truth is expressed with these words: 'Being justified freely by his grace' (Rom. 3:24). Surely this proves that justification is entirely free, without the least regard to any qualities in, or works performed by, the sinner. Words could not be clearer. The word 'freely' in the original means 'without cause' and describes the character of those who are justified. This shows that our works in no way 'cause' our justification. The same word is used in reference to our Lord: 'They hated me without a cause' (John 15:25; Ps. 69:4). Just as there was no cause in Jesus for the hatred of the Jews, so there is no cause in the sinner for God to justify him. Nothing in him or about him is taken into account when God bestows this bless-ing. There are no conditions to perform, no terms to be ful-filled, no good qualities to be obtained in order to be justified. Justification is a glorious blessing of pure grace. This is how every true believer esteems it and, as such, rejoices in it. In this, as in every other part of salvation, he is willing to be nothing, even less than nothing, that grace may reign and be all in all.

Our pardon is free

We can also show that justification is all of grace, by considering the freeness of our pardon. Justification and pardon are dis-tinct blessings and yet cannot be separated. Those who are pardoned are justified, and those who are justified are pardoned. This means that if our pardon is free, our justification cannot be conditional upon our works. I dealt with the freeness of our pardon in the previous chapter and so will not repeat myself now. These things must silence the fears of those who are guilty and accursed and self-condemned. May their hopes be raised by beholding the glory of the one who is absolutely just and yet the *justifier of the ungodly*.

We must now consider how it is possible that the condemned criminal may be honourably acquitted by God and accepted as righteous. Here we will see that God's holiness and justice harmonize perfectly with his tender mercy and free favour. It cannot be otherwise. The Judge of all the earth must do right (Gen. 18:25). He cannot acquit anybody without a perfect righteousness. To justify is to pronounce as righteous. Justification is a legal term and denotes a judicial act. If a person were to be justified without a righteousness, the judgement would not be according to truth; the sentence would be false and unrighteous.

Perfect righteousness required

The righteousness by which we are justified must be perfect. It must be equal to the demands of the law and acceptable to the sovereign Judge. It is obvious that every judge must have a rule by which to carry out his judicial function. This rule is the law. To talk about passing judgement without reference to the law is absurd and contradictory. To judge a person in court is to determine whether he has broken the law or not. The judge considers the facts and compares them with the law, that is, the rule of action. He then pronounces the person's conduct to be right or wrong and passes sentence accordingly. God requires complete conformity to his law. Therefore, an imperfect obedience is not righteousness in his sight. In his capacity as a righteous Judge, he cannot accept anything short of the rule. The Lord has said that he will 'by no means clear the guilty' (Exod. 34:7). This means that he will justify no one without a perfect righteousness. This righteousness must meet the demands of

God's law. It must honour his justice and truth. It must give the sinner a perfect standing before the Lord and an assurance of eternal happiness in heaven.

Many people talk about *conditions* of justification but differ as to what they believe these conditions are. It is clear that there is only one condition of our acceptance with God and that is a perfect righteousness. This is what both the law and the gospel require. Those who think that anything less than perfect obedience is accepted by God do great dishonour to him and his law. The gospel in no way makes void the law. On the contrary, the gospel and the death of Christ demonstrate that Jehovah is absolutely inflexible in the demands of his law. The way in which sinners are justified does not infringe at all on its rights. In its moral aspect, God's law is unalterable and eternal. In the Garden of Eden, Adam was required to obey it perfectly as a condition of life. Though in a state of apostasy, we are still required to do the same. The law must be fulfilled perfectly, either by us or a surety, if we are to be justified and not fall eternally under its curse.

Law will condemn us

Where shall we find and how shall we obtain a righteousness which justifies? Shall we look to the law for help? Shall we apply ourselves with diligence and zeal to obey God's commandments? To do this would certainly flatter our pride but would betray our ignorance, disappoint our hopes and lead to eternal ruin. The apostle Paul says specifically that 'by the deeds of the law no flesh will be justified in his sight' (Rom. 3:20). The deeds of the law are those works of piety and humanity that the law requires. The law demands a perfect love to both God and man. This is why the Apostle excludes our works from having anything to do with our justification. In fact, he goes on to say that 'by the law is the knowledge of sin'. The law shows how we have departed from God's revealed will and deserve its everlasting curse. Far from pronouncing us righteous in God's sight, the law proves us guilty! It is impossible to be justified by law. As Paul says: 'The law entered that the offence might abound' (Rom. 5:20). This means that the law was given at Mount Sinai in order to reveal both the vast number and the seriousness of our sins. Furthermore, the Apostle says that 'the law brings about wrath' (Rom. 4:15). It reveals the wrath of God against all ungodliness and unrighteousness of men. It declares the sinner to be guilty. Far from justifying anyone, it announces utter destruction against the sinner and unsheathes the sword of God's vengeance.

Again Paul says, 'For as many as are of the works of the law are under the curse; for it is written, "Cursed is everyone who does not continue in all things which are written in the book of the law, to do them"' (Gal. 3:10). We learn that those who try their best to keep the law, far from being on the way to acceptance with God, are under a dreadful curse. It is impossible to find acceptance with God without an obedience that is in complete conformity to the law in thought, word and deed all of the time. Those who stumble at one point break the whole law, are guilty before God and are exposed to ruin (James 2:10).

Faith and law are in opposition

To prove his point, Paul shows that living by faith and living by the works of the law are contrary to each other. These are his words: 'But that no one is justified by the law in the sight of God is evident, for "The just shall live by faith." Yet the law is not of faith, but "The man who does them shall live by them"' (Gal. 3:11-12). The Apostle teaches that no one, however excellent his moral character, can be justified by keeping the law. He says that the law is not of faith; it makes no mention of a Redeemer or of believing in him. The language of the law is 'doing' rather than 'believing' and that only he who obeys all the law shall find acceptance and enjoy peace.

Writing under the inspiration of the Spirit, Paul argues elsewhere in this way: 'If righteousness comes through the law, then Christ died in vain' (Gal. 2:21). If we are justified by our works then why did Jesus come and die? What a shocking conclusion! It would mean that Christ's obedience and death were useless and quite unnecessary. Again Paul says, 'For if those who are of the law are heirs, faith is made void and the promise made of no effect' (Rom. 4:14). This means that, if those who rely on their works are accepted by God, then faith in a dying Redeemer is pointless and the promise of life through him is empty.

When Paul excludes the works of the law from our justification, he is not thinking only of the ceremonial aspects of the law. These were the temporary institutions of the old covenant, which have now been abrogated by the death of Christ. Paul's purpose is to set aside all obedience to every law. He excludes all works of every kind from our justification.

Expanding on the verse quoted above, Paul shows that the law stands in direct opposition to the righteousness of faith: 'For the promise that he would be the heir of the world was not to Abraham or to his seed through the law, but through the righteousness of faith. For if those who are of the law are heirs, faith is made void and the promise made of no effect, because the law brings about wrath; for where there is no law there is no transgression. Therefore it is of faith that it might be according to grace, so that the promise might be sure to all the seed' (Rom. 4:13-16). It is apparent that the Apostle has the moral law and not the ceremonial law in mind here. The ceremonial law did reveal in various ways the grace of God in the gospel. In these types and shadows believers saw something of the promised Messiah and received life through him. It is the moral law which is 'not of faith'. In the law there is no grace, nothing for sinners to trust and hope in and no promises made to them. Quite the reverse is true because the law 'brings about wrath'. When the law is transgressed, God's wrath is incurred and a sense of that wrath is known in the conscience where there is conviction of sin.

These things can only be applied to the moral law. The ceremonial law has now been abrogated for the Jews, and the Gentiles were never required to obey it anyway. However, all mankind has broken the moral law. Paul even speaks of his own experience in this way: 'I would not have known covetousness unless the law had said, "You shall not covet"' (Rom. 7:7). It is clear what law the apostle is thinking of here and he shows that the moral law is spiritual in demanding purity of thought and affection. Elsewhere he says: 'For by grace you have been saved through faith, and that not of yourselves; it is the gift of God, not of works, lest anyone should boast' (Eph. 2:8-9). 'To demonstrate at the present time his righteousness, that he might be just and the justifier of the one who has faith in Jesus. Where is boasting then? It is excluded. By what law? Of works? No, but by the law of faith. Therefore we conclude that a man is justified by faith apart from the deeds of the law' (Rom. 3:26-28). Paul shows that nobody has any grounds for boasting although men are so prone to feel proud of their moral goodness and sincere intentions. We see that all works, whether moral or ceremonial, are excluded from our justification.

Faith is not righteousness

Furthermore, we are not to think of our faith itself as our righteousness or as the reason why we are justified. Believers are said to be justified *by* faith, not *for* faith. We can show that faith is not our righteousness in many ways. Nobody's faith is perfect and even if it was, it could not be equal to the demands of

God's law. Perfect faith cannot be regarded as a complete righteousness. The obedience by which a sinner is justified is called 'the righteousness of God through faith' and 'righteousness by faith' and is described as being 'revealed ... to faith' (Rom. 3:22; Phil. 3:9; Rom. 1:17). Clearly, it cannot be faith itself.

In the matter of being justified, faith is opposed to all works. 'To him who does not work but believes... ' (Rom. 4:5). However, if faith is our righteousness it must be considered as a work or a condition upon which our acceptance with God is suspended. It would also follow that some believers are more justified than others because there are various degrees of faith (Matt. 6:30; Luke 7:9). It is absurd to suggest that some are more accepted by God due to the strength of their faith. The righteousness by which many are justified is said to be the obedience of the 'one' (Rom. 5:15-19). We cannot be justified for the sake of our faith because there would then be many different 'righteousnesses'. It would also mean that we could, with pride, depend upon and rejoice in our faith as that which God has appointed for our righteousness. We could plead our faith before him at the throne of grace and regard it as the foundation of our eternal happiness. In this way, faith and not Christ is the most important thing and that to which we must look. The glorious Redeemer then takes a secondary place in our justification and our faith becomes everything.

Some have said that Scripture teaches that our faith is accepted by God as our righteousness. They point to Abraham and the way in which he is said to have been justified (Gen. 15:6; Rom. 4:3, 9). To understand the words 'faith was accounted to Abraham for righteousness' in this way is to contradict Paul's whole argument in dealing with the justification of sinners. His main purpose is to show that justification is free; that God justifies without any cause in the creature. However, according to this view, faith *is* the condition, the cause, the basis upon which we are accepted as righteous. It is not faith in itself which justifies us but the glorious *object* of our faith. This is what Paul is teaching.

Is sincere obedience enough?

It has been suggested that the law in all its strictness has now been abrogated because of Christ's work as Mediator and that a new law has been introduced which is adapted more easily to the weaknesses of sinners. Men are incapable of perfect obedience but God only now requires an obedience that is sincere for acceptance by him. So it is thought. Such an idea presents the gospel making void the law and this is contrary to Scripture (Rom. 3:31). This also means that the original law was too strict in its precepts and too severe in its penalty. How abhorrent this view is because the law is described as being 'holy and just and good' (Rom. 7:12). This also calls into question the wisdom, justice and goodness of God. It means that he gave a law which he then had to repeal in order to accomplish his plan of grace. We have already seen that an imperfect righteousness cannot justify us before God. Yet this 'new law' requires an imperfect obedience and therefore even this cannot justify us before our eternal Judge.

We are not accepted by God because of any holiness wrought in us by the Holy Spirit or any good works which we have performed with the help of God's grace after regeneration. Even these things must still be regarded as our own righteousness because they are done by us. Furthermore, they are still imperfect and so cannot justify us. The apostle Paul shows clearly that even these good works have no bearing on our justification (Eph. 2:8-10).

To assert that our own righteousness is the condition of justification is to confuse the two opposite covenants of works and grace. The covenant of works was that arrangement which required personal obedience as the condition of life and acceptance with God. The language of this covenant is 'Do this and live.' In this covenant, blessings are not given by way of grace but by way of reward and debt (Rom. 4:4). The other covenant of which Scripture speaks is all of grace. It is a covenant of absolute promises with no conditions to be fulfilled (Eph. 2:12; Jer. 31:31-34; Heb. 8:10-12). The blessings of this covenant, including a justifying righteousness, are received by faith alone and not works.

The imputed righteousness of Jesus

We have shown that God will not and cannot justify anyone without a perfect righteousness. Such a righteousness cannot be found in our own works or our faith or in the fruit of the Holy Spirit in our hearts and lives. Where can we possibly find the righteousness we need? Only in Jesus Christ and his finished work as our substitute. The spotless obedience, the bitter sufferings and the accursed death of our heavenly Surety constitute the very righteousness by which sinners are justified before God. It is this righteousness alone that the eternal Sovereign accepts and the basis upon which he will pronounce the sinner just. We are said to be made righteous by the obedience of Christ and to be justified by his blood (Rom. 5:19, 9). The obedience and blood of Christ are put to the sinner's account, so much so that the sinner is regarded as having obeyed and suffered himself. Christ's work for sinners is the only basis upon which we are pronounced righteous with a right to life by the God who is of 'purer eyes than to behold evil' (Hab. 1:13).

It is evident from Scripture that we are justified by an imputed rather than a personal righteousness. Nothing could be clearer. In this way Jehovah justified Abraham, the Father of the faithful. The nation of Israel originated with Abraham and he was honoured by being called 'the friend of God' (James 2:23). The apostle Paul holds him up as an example of God's grace in justification. This was partly to convict Paul's fellow Jews who were seeking to be justified by works.

The example of Abraham

Abraham was a great man who is renowned for his faith and obedience to God. Very few saints have ever shown such a cheerful submission to God's will and such confidence in God's promises. As soon as God told him to leave his country and father's house, Abraham 'obeyed ... and went out, not knowing where he was going' (Heb. 11:8). As soon as the Lord told him to sacrifice his only son Isaac, whom he loved, he obeyed in spite of the many difficulties surrounding God's will in this. Yet these things, though highly pleasing to God, were not the cause or condition of his justification. These works showed that Abraham's faith was real and that his piety was genuine. In this sense he was justified, or declared righteous, by his works (James 2:21-24). Paul shows that Abraham's works were not the basis upon which he was accepted by God: 'For if Abraham was justified by works, he has something to boast about, but not before God. For what does the Scripture say? "Abraham believed God, and it was accounted to him for righteousness" ... Now it was not written for his sake alone that it was imputed to him, but also for us. It shall be imputed to us who believe in him who raised up Jesus our Lord from the dead' (Rom. 4:2-3, 23-24). 'So then those who are of faith are blessed with believing Abraham' (Gal. 3:9). If a person of such victorious faith, exalted piety and amazing obedience as Abraham did not obtain acceptance with God by his works but by an imputed righteousness, what hope is there for those who endeavour to be justified by works which cannot compare with those of Jehovah's friend?

The example of 'the blessed man'

To illustrate this truth Paul then refers to the words David used
to describe the truly 'blessed man'. How does the royal psalm-
ist describe this man? To what does he attribute his acceptance
with God? Is it a personal or imputed righteousness? Does David
represent him as attaining such a happy condition through his
own sincere obedience in keeping God's law to the best of his
ability? By no means. His words are: 'Blessed are those whose
lawless deeds are forgiven, and whose sins are covered; blessed
is the man to whom the LORD shall not impute sin' (Rom. 4:7-8;
Ps. 32:1-2). The blessed man is here described as one who is,
in himself, polluted with sin and guilty of breaking God's law.
Before grace made a difference he was as unworthy and vile as
the rest of mankind but the inspired writer informs us that all his
blessedness arises from an imputed righteousness. This can be
the only meaning of Paul's words: 'Just as David also describes
the blessedness of the man to whom God imputes righteousness apart from works' (Rom. 4:6).

This righteousness cannot be a person's own obedience because it is expressly said to be *apart from works*. His own virtues
and duties, however excellent, contribute nothing towards it.
No; it is perfect in itself and completely separate from everything he has done or can do. The phraseology of the inspired
writer is very remarkable. He not only speaks of blessedness as
a result of an imputed righteousness, but he also describes the
obedience which is applied to the sinner, as being *apart from
works*. He does this to defend the truth in a more powerful way
and to secure the honour of grace more effectively. Paul wrote
of an 'imputed righteousness', a 'righteousness apart from the
law' and a 'righteousness apart from works'. This was the doctrine he preached and this was the faith of the early church.

In these days, sadly, these phrases are discarded as obsolete
and offensive by many who call themselves Christians. They

regard those who use such phrases frequently as being somewhat fanatical in their thinking. The truth of an imputed righteousness is rejected with contempt because it is thought to be insulting to common sense. In spite of these things, the great Apostle considered it as being intimately connected with the happiness of mankind and esteemed the blessing as the only solid basis of all our hope and comfort.

The example of the apostle Paul

We have seen what Paul says about the justification of Abraham and his application of David's description of the blessed man, but what was the foundation of his own eternal happiness? On what righteousness did he rely? The teacher of God's infallible word gives the answer to us in the following passage: 'Yet indeed I also count all things loss for the excellence of the knowledge of Christ Jesus my Lord, for whom I have suffered the loss of all things, and count them as rubbish, that I may gain Christ and be found in him, not having my own righteousness, which is from the law, but that which is through faith in Christ, the righteousness which is from God by faith' (Phil. 3:8-9). Here we learn that Paul esteemed his privileges of birth, his pharisaical zeal, his submission to ceremonial rites and performance of moral duties as *loss*.

He also regarded all of his works since conversion as having no worth in the important matter of acceptance with God. Although these things were useful and notable when considered in their proper place, compared with the *excellence of the knowledge of Christ Jesus* they are not only little or nothing but *loss* itself. Such was Paul's love for his Saviour and dependence upon his righteousness that he had cheerfully suffered the loss of all the things which he had valued so highly. Such was his estimation of his own performances when compared with the righteousness of Christ that he counted them as *rubbish* or as offal which is only fit to be thrown to the dogs. Paul's chief desire and supreme concern was to *win Christ* in order that his every need might be supplied and that he might be made completely happy. He desired that when the Judge ascends the throne at the final judgement, when all nations appear before him, when none but the perfectly righteous are able to stand, that he would be *found in him* the Beloved, as the Lord his righteousness. By this Paul explains that he was not depending upon his own righteousness which is of the law but upon the righteousness which is through faith in Christ. Paul was not even prepared to trust in the righteous deeds that he had performed as a Christian. He did not depend upon his obedience to the law as a rule of conduct, even by the influence of grace as the principle of his spiritual life. His only trust was the righteousness that was finished by Christ, revealed in the gospel and received by faith; the obedience that was performed by the incarnate Son and that is most excellent, *the righteousness which is from God by faith.*

The Apostle's purpose in this passage is to show in what a sinner can safely trust and what is an acceptable ground of rejoicing. He intimates that there can be no confidence towards God, no acceptance with him and consequently no cause of spiritual joy without a righteousness. Condemnation and wrath must be our portion if we appear in our sins before the righteous Judge. According to Paul there is a two-fold righteousness. The one he calls our own, which is from the law; and the one he describes as the righteousness of God, which is through faith in Christ. Paul signifies that these are entirely distinct, and far from working together in our justification, they are completely opposite to each other. In seeking acceptance with the Most High, he who embraces the one must reject the other. In fact, all mankind rely on one or the other. He makes it very clear which of the two was the ground of his confidence and the source of his joy. However much the Judaizing teachers, of whom he speaks in the beginning of the chapter, might put their confidence in the flesh in relying on their own works, the Apostle was determined to adopt a very different method and to seek for acceptance in a different way. Having warned them of their danger and guarded the Philippians against these destructive errors, Paul declares that the righteousness which he deemed sufficient was not his own and was not of the law. It was a gift of grace received through faith in Christ. By this he means the obedience which our Lord performed as a surety. This was the object of Paul's dependence and in this alone he gloried.

As the Apostle considered the purity of God's law and the majesty of the eternal Judge before whom he would stand one day, he realized that his own righteousness was completely useless. He rejected it with disdain and poured contempt upon it in calling it 'loss' and 'rubbish'. Such was the experience and the hope of that wonderful man, whose apostolic gifts and Christian graces, whose ministerial usefulness and exemplary conduct, rendered him an eminent blessing to the world and an honour to the great Redeemer's cause.

There are many arguments that might be presented from God's unerring Word in order to prove this wonderful and comforting doctrine. I shall confine myself to the few that follow. It has already been proved that the subject of justification is an *ungodly* person. Therefore, his pardon and acceptance cannot be the result of his own obedience. It is equally clear that *as* an ungodly person he cannot be justified. He must stand right in the eye of the law and unreprovable before his Judge, before he can be acquitted in judgement. It follows that this can only happen by the righteousness of another. Where is such a righteousness to be found? Not in the obedience of our fellow creatures who have been justified. This would be the discredited Roman Catholic teaching of supererogation (the earning of extra merit that can be drawn upon in prayer by the sinner). Not in the sanctity of angels, for they are not responsible for us. Not in God's essential righteousness because this cannot be communicated to mere creatures. This righteousness can only be found in Christ. It is his complete conformity to the holy law as a voluntary substitute for the ungodly. In what way can this righteousness be applied to us except by imputation? This must be the case since the person justified is ungodly in himself and since the Judge of all the earth cannot justify without a righteousness.

Christ's righteousness justifies us

In handling this wonderful teaching, Paul says that Adam was a 'type of him who was to come' (Rom. 5:14). He is, of course, referring to the Lord Messiah. Paul forms a striking comparison between the first and second Adam; between the disobedience of one and the obedience of the other, together with the effects of each. He represents Adam as a public person, as the constituted federal head of all his posterity, and Christ as representative of all his chosen seed. He signifies that the first offence of the former was imputed to all his natural offspring and that the perfect obedience of the latter is imputed to all his spiritual seed. By the imputation of that offence all mankind were 'made sinners'. They came under a charge of guilt and the awful sentence of condemnation to eternal death. By the imputation of Christ's obedience all who believe are 'made righteous'. They are acquitted from every legal charge and adjudged to eternal life. As it was the one offence of one man that brought death and misery on all the human race, so it is by the righteousness of one man, even the Lord from heaven, that spiritual life and eternal happiness are brought in (Rom. 5:18-19). It is clear that Adam's act of disobeying God's commandment was imputed

to his offspring before they were guilty of any actual transgression
of their own. The basis of this imputation was their natural
relation to Adam as their federal head. It follows that what is
imputed to believers is the complete performance of God's precepts by our Lord Jesus Christ, that is, his actual conformity to
the holy law. By this excellent righteousness, all who believe
are justified and entitled to immortal glory, without any good
works of their own and before they have performed any acceptable duty. In whatever way Adam's sin was made ours to
condemnation, in the same way the righteousness of his glorious Antitype is made ours to justification. If the former was by
imputation, then so is the latter.

He was made sin for us

The momentous truth for which I am pleading is also taught in
the following passage: 'For he made him who knew no sin to
be sin for us, that we might become the righteousness of God
in him' (2 Cor. 5:21). It is clear that as Christ the Surety was
made sin, so we are made righteousness. In the very same way
in which our sins were made his, his obedience becomes ours.
In what sense was the Holy One of God made sin? Why was he
punished as one guilty of breaking the law of God? How could
he become an atoning sacrifice for sin? It is absurd and blasphemous to suggest that sin was infused into him so as to reside
in him. Paul must mean that Christ was made sin by imputation. This was the way in which our adorable Surety came
under a charge of guilt. It must follow, by necessary consequence and in order to preserve Paul's beautiful antithesis, that
those who are truly righteous are made so by imputation and
imputation only. For as it is impossible that any person, being
perfectly innocent, should be made sin except by having the
sins of others placed to his account or charged upon them in a
judicial way; so those that are in themselves guilty cannot be

made righteous in somebody else, by his obedience, without having it imputed to them. As the blessed Jesus is said to be made sin, so we are said to be made righteous. Just as it was not through any criminal conduct of his own that he became sin; so it is not by any pious activity of ours that we become righteous. As it was not on account of any evil qualities infused into Christ that he was treated as an offender by God's justice, so it is not by virtue of any holiness wrought in us that we are accepted and treated as righteous. As that sin for which Jesus was condemned and punished was not found in him but charged upon him, so that righteousness by which we are justified and entitled to happiness is not inherent in us but imputed to us.

Our works are futile

The objections which the Apostle answers and the way in which he refutes them when handling the doctrine of justification also strongly imply that his purpose was to completely exclude all the works of every law and all duties of every kind in our acceptance with God. His concern was to show that this can only be by pure grace and an imputed righteousness. Some have objected that the method of justification set forth by Paul is not only detrimental to holiness of life but overthrows all morality. Paul was accused of making void God's law; of encouraging believers to continue in sin because they were not under the law and to multiply transgressions that grace may abound and to do evil that good might come (Rom. 3:31; 6:15; 6:1; 3:8). It follows that if Paul had taught or given the slightest intimation that righteous deeds, or holy inclinations, were in any way necessary to a sinner's justification, then the apostolic gospel would not have been charged with such terrible consequences. The enemies of sacred truth would not have had the slightest opportunity to malign his doctrine as leading to licentiousness. The fact that they do so shows that Paul exhorted sinners to renounce all human obedience and to place their whole dependence on the work and worthiness of Christ alone.

Our obedience is futile

It is possible that some, through ignorance or prejudice, have misunderstood Paul's meaning of rejecting all holy desires and pious endeavours from that righteousness by which we are justified. Perhaps he only meant to exclude a spurious kind of holiness and works of a particular sort. Perhaps he rejected only the works of the ceremonial law or works performed prior to regeneration without the aid of God's grace. Perhaps he left room for an evangelical obedience to be part of our acceptance with God. We find that Paul nowhere seeks to correct such misunderstandings by distinguishing between works that contribute to our justification and those which do not. He excluded completely all duties and works of men without exception.

Paul's answer to those who say, 'Shall we continue in sin that grace may abound?' is 'Certainly not! How shall we who died to sin live any longer in it?' (Rom. 6:1-2). By this he means that those who are the subjects of grace and believe in Christ, being dead to sin, cannot walk in the ways of ungodliness. For them to do so would be absolutely inconsistent with their new state and with that principle of spiritual life which they have received. However, Paul does not give the slightest intimation of the necessity of holiness or obedience to gain the favour of God and procure acceptance with him. There are some people who are sure that their doctrine of justification is the same as Paul's but believe that some holiness or personal moral goodness is necessary to be justified by God. Could these people be accused of teaching a doctrine that leads to licentiousness? Could they be charged with making the law void and of encouraging others to do evil that good may come? Of course not! This strongly implies that the doctrines they hold to are not the same

that Paul preached, and which the early church professed. All
of this shows that natural men are as incapable of discerning
spiritual things and are just as hostile towards the genuine gospel
now as in apostolic times.

Free gift of God

The righteousness by which we are justified is a free gift. This is
clear from the expression 'the gift of righteousness' (Rom. 5:17).
Paul also states in this verse that believers receive it rather than
perform it. The gospel of sovereign grace, which proclaims its
sufficiency, suitability and freeness, is called 'the word of righteousness' and 'the ministry of righteousness' (Heb. 5:13; 2 Cor.
3:9). One of the glorious names which our divine Surety bears
is 'The Lord our Righteousness' (Jer. 23:6). In perfect harmony
with this, Christ is said to be righteousness from God for believers and they are said to be made the righteousness of God in
him (1 Cor. 1:30; 2 Cor. 5:21). Believers are declared by the
infallible Spirit to be justified in him; accepted in him; complete
in him; and saved in him (Isa. 45:25; Eph. 1:6; Col. 2:10; Isa.
45:17). This is the God-appointed method of justification and
the provision made by grace for the final acceptance of guilty,
ungodly and wretched creatures.

Revealed in the gospel

The grand design of the gospel is to reveal this righteousness of
God (Rom. 1:16-17). It is to display the riches of that grace
which provided and bestows freely this wonderful gift. The
gospel informs us that, with regard to justification, what is required of the transgressor in terms of doing and suffering, was
performed by our adorable Substitute. It is the place of true
faith, not to regard itself as a condition of acceptance with God,
nor to assert its own importance, nor to share the glory with

our Saviour's righteousness, but to receive it as absolutely sufficient to justify freely the most ungodly sinner. For what is evangelical faith but receiving Christ and his righteousness? (Isa. 45:22; John 1:12; Col. 2:6; Rom. 1:17; 5:17).

In Christ alone

In other words, this faith is a dependence on Jesus alone for eternal salvation. Such a faith is completely sufficient to save the most guilty, supply the wants of the most needy and freely save the vilest of sinners. As the object of faith is the divine Redeemer and his finished work, and the warrant and ground of faith is the report of the gospel, we can say that the act of faith is to trust entirely and without reserve on the faithful word which God has spoken and on the perfect work which Christ has wrought. This is the faith of God's elect and the evidences of its truth and reality are love to God and a holy obedience to him, peace of conscience and a hope of glory. To a greater or lesser degree, these are the proper effects and genuine fruits of faith.

Complete acceptance with God

How supremely happy must be those who have been justified by God's grace! They have all been pronounced righteous by the eternal Judge. There is nothing to be laid to their charge. They are acquitted in a way that honours all the perfections of deity and are everlastingly free from condemnation. Though their sins are both numerous and loathsome, they are purged away by atoning blood and their souls are clothed with that most excellent robe of the Redeemer's righteousness. In this sense they are already in God's sight without 'spot or wrinkle or any such thing' (Eph. 5:27). Believers are 'presented' by

their great Representative, 'in the body of his flesh through death
... holy, and blameless, and above reproach' in the sight of
Omniscience (Col. 1:22). They are fair as the purest wool and
whiter than the snow. Let believers rejoice in the thought that
the work and worth of the Lord Redeemer gives them acceptance with infinite majesty and dignity before the angels of light.

A sure foundation

They have consolation on earth and estimation in heaven. They
shall stand with courage at the bar of judgement and appear
with honour among the inhabitants of glory. Let the legalist
boast of his good works and devout services and strict holiness. The man who is taught by God esteems them all, if set in
competition with Christ or presuming to stand in the place of
his righteousness, as sordid as dross, as vile as dung, as lighter
than vanity and worse than nothing. If he had the meekness of
Moses, the patience of Job, the zeal of Paul and love of John,
he would not and dare not advance the least claim to justification and eternal life on the basis of these things. It is only in
the righteousness of the blessed Jesus that he dares to confide.
It is only in his obedience that he glories. This obedience is an
immovable basis for the anxious mind to rest upon by faith.
This is a sure foundation to support the believer's hope of glory,
even when he views God's righteous law in its full extent and
purity. This confidence will support the soul nearing death, which
will soon enter an eternal world. Such is the perfection and
power of this righteousness that it will not fail as the awesome
Day of Judgement draws near. Grace reigns in freely bestowing
this righteousness and in our complete justification by it.

Praise and glory to our Saviour

Let us then look to the imputed righteousness of Christ. Let us
rely on it and glory in it. This righteousness is full of dignity and

is freely available to us in our need. What an encouraging thought this is! This way of justification has the effect of pulling down the pride of the self-righteous professor of religion, who considers himself as standing upon better terms with his Maker than his ungodly neighbour. It also raises the drooping spirits of the trembling sinner who has nothing to plead as to why sentence of condemnation, already pronounced upon him, should not be executed in all its rigour. If we could not look to Christ's obedience until we were conscious of having some righteousness of our own, we would be left discouraged and despairing because damnation would be certain. However, this righteousness, and justification by it, is perfectly free for the worst of sinners. Thanks be to God for this unparalleled favour! For the works of every law, in every sense, as performed by man, are entirely excluded from having any concern in our acceptance with God. Therefore, since it is in Christ alone, as our head, representative and surety, that we are or can be justified, he alone should have all the glory. He is infinitely worthy to have the unrivalled honour. In the light of all this, let the very worst of sinners trust in the obedience of the dying Jesus, as being absolutely sufficient to justify him, without good works or duties, without good habits or qualities, however performed or acquired. God has declared in his Word of Truth that he will never be disappointed.

Honour and joy for believers

Here is full relief and immediate comfort for all who have ruined themselves by their numerous sins and provocations. Here a complete righteousness is revealed. In this righteousness you can see that God is just and yet the justifier of the ungodly. It is true that if God were only just, then only misery could be expected by the guilty. However, God is not only a righteous Judge but a compassionate Saviour. This draws us to God for it speaks of deliverance and administers consolation. Though you have no righteousness, yet the wisdom of God has appointed a way and the infinite riches of sovereign grace have provided effectual means for your full discharge before the great tribunal. This way provides you with honour and joy beyond your highest comprehension and shall make you happy to all eternity.

Are you oppressed with guilt and harassed with fears of deserved ruin? Are you weary with seeking to establish your own righteousness? (Rom. 10:3). Are you aware that you are unworthy and have nothing to recommend you to the Redeemer? Remember that no recommendation is needed and that nothing is required of you for such a purpose. 'Come and take *freely*' is what Jesus says (Rev. 22:17). He has all that you want, however impoverished you are. He gives all with the most liberal hand. Let the fact that 'grace reigns' be your encouragement when thinking about acceptance with Christ and your justification in him before the Almighty.

In conclusion

In the light of all that has been said, perhaps you still think it wise and safe to depend on your own righteousness. Let me remind you of the absolute purity and infinite holiness, the transcendent majesty and awful glories of that God to whom you must give an account and before whom you must soon appear. Remember that your supreme Judge has terrible royal power.

He is 'of purer eyes than to behold evil, and cannot look on wickedness' (Hab. 1:13). He will by no means clear the guilty (Exod. 34:7). God is a 'consuming fire' (Heb. 12:29). His righteous judgement is that those who sin are 'deserving of death' (Rom. 1:32). The law of God pronounces an awful curse on every offender. Remember that he, whose divine prerogative it is to justify, is a 'jealous God' (Exod. 20:5). He is jealous of his honour as a righteous governor and he is determined to support the rights of his throne. So terrible is his indignation that once his wrath is kindled, it will consume every false refuge to which sinners flee and 'burn to the lowest hell' (Deut. 32:22). So awful is Jehovah in his majesty that before him the 'mountains quake' and the 'pillars of heaven tremble and are astonished at his rebuke' (Nahum 1:5; Job 26:11). As his condescending smile irradiates the countenance of angels and crowns them with unutterable bliss, so his righteous frown is nothing less than absolute destruction. So flaming is his purity and so dazzling his glory, that 'even the moon does not shine, and the stars are not pure in his sight' (Job 25:5). In his presence the seraphim, those most exalted of mere creatures, cover their faces and their feet in profound humiliation as they cry in responsive strains, 'Holy, holy, holy is the LORD of hosts' (Isa. 6:2-3).

In the light of these things we ask the same question that Bildad asked: 'How then can man be righteous before God? Or how can he be pure who is born of a woman?' (Job 25:4). How will you answer him whose eyes are a flame of fire and whose particular province it is to search the human heart and explore its hidden evils? To what refuge will you flee when he sifts your conduct and marks your offences? By trusting in your own duties, you slight the great atonement of Christ and despise his revealed righteousness. Christ shall profit you nothing (Gal. 5:2).

You may talk in lofty strains about man's moral excellence, the dignity of human nature, the worth of personal obedience and the efficacy of penitential tears. You may proclaim the necessity of good works and reject with disdain the doctrine of imputed righteousness. You can do all of this but only while your conscience is unaffected by the sight of God's purity and the sense of his holy presence. As soon as you begin to form your ideas of God from the inspired Scriptures rather than your own imagination, your pretensions to personal worthiness must subside and your mouth must be stopped. If not completely silent, you must exclaim, 'Who is able to stand before this holy LORD God?' (1 Sam. 6:20). If you then find no immediate relief from Christ's atoning death, you will be ready to add, 'Who among us shall dwell with the devouring fire? Who among us shall dwell with everlasting burnings?' (Isa. 33:14).

Before the judgement seat of Christ

We are directed by the Holy Spirit speaking in the Scriptures to conceive of justification as *before* God and *in his sight* (Rom. 4:2; 3:20). This intimates that when we consider acceptance with God we should see ourselves as in the immediate presence of the one who will soon ascend the great white throne in order to pass an irreversible sentence upon all of his creatures. We should consider on what ground we shall be able to stand in front of the Eternal Judge before whose face heaven and earth shall flee away (Rev. 20:11). The only way to avoid deceiving yourself in such a matter of vast importance is to consider yourself before the judgement seat of Christ. In what righteousness dare you trust then? Remember that your everlasting fate depends upon this. How you plead before God will determine whether you will enjoy eternal happiness or suffer eternal misery. You should anticipate, in your own meditations, that great decisive day and ask your conscience, 'On what shall I then depend? What shall I dare to plead when, with astonishment, I behold my Judge?' It is sheer folly to rely on any obedience now as the means of your justification, which you would not be prepared to plead on the Day of Judgement.

Confession of sins

Consider the way in which the greatest saints and holiest men have sincerely acknowledged and confessed their impurity and sinfulness before the one who is 'glorious in holiness' (Exod.

15:11). Job was an eminent saint and had no equal on earth according to God's own testimony. He was conscious of his integrity and avowed it before men. He vindicated his exemplary conduct against the accusations of his critical friends. However, when the Almighty addressed Job, he said not a word about his inherent uprightness or pious performances. In the language of deepest abasement he exclaimed, 'Behold, I am vile' (Job 40:4); 'I abhor myself and repent in dust and ashes' (Job 42:6). David, the man after God's own heart, made it his earnest request that God would not enter into judgement with him (Ps. 143:2). He was well aware that neither he nor any other living soul could be justified by means of his own obedience. In order to rebuke the pride of self-righteous confidence, with emotions of holy reverence and sacred awe, David asks, 'If you, LORD, should mark iniquities, O Lord, who could stand?' (Ps. 130:3). Isaiah was an eminent prophet and distinguished servant of God and yet, when he beheld Jehovah's glory and heard the seraphim proclaim his holiness, loudly exclaimed, 'Woe is me, for I am undone! Because I am a man of unclean lips' (Isa. 6:5). His distress was not removed nor was his conscience relieved, until pardon through the atonement was applied to him.

Put on Christ's righteousness

Is it wise or safe for you to trust in your imperfect duties, when persons of such eminent character and exalted piety acknowledged these things and had such views of themselves and their attainments? If *their* personal obedience could not bear the divine scrutiny, what could we say of *your* personal obedience before the God who searches every heart? If Jehovah charges his angels with error and if the heavens are not pure in his sight, what can be said of man who is abominable and filthy and who drinks iniquity like water? (Job 4:18; 15:15-16). Between human obedience and angelic holiness, there is no more comparison than between a clod of the field and a star in the firmament. Yet, proud man would presume to be righteous, though vile with sin and exposed to ruin. Although many think so highly of their own obedience, the sinner whose conscience is pressed with a sense of guilt and every true Christian will dread appearing in their own righteousness before the final Judge. The man who is taught of God would rather the rocks cover him and he lose his existence than to appear before the Most High in the filthy rags of his own duties or in any righteousness but that which is perfect and divine.

The reign of grace

Chapter 7

The reign of grace in our adoption

'By the privilege of adoption we are invested with such a character and brought into such a state as to make us fit to join with the saints and angels in glory. Only omnipotent, reigning grace could be sufficient to effect such a change.'

7.

The reign of grace in our adoption

Those whom God has justified and admitted into a state of reconciliation with himself, he has also adopted as his children. By virtue of adoption, believers have an indisputable right of inheritance, which consists in all the blessings of grace and riches of glory to come. The word *adoption* signifies that act *by which a person takes the child of another, not related to him, into his family and entitles him to the privileges of his own son.* In the Greek and Roman states it was customary for a wealthy man with no children of his own to choose somebody else upon whom he would put his name and proclaim him publicly as his heir. The person adopted would have to relinquish his own family, never to return to it again. He would be legally entitled to the inheritance upon the death of the one who had adopted him. Though he previously had no claim to this or any possible hope of obtaining it, yet adoption has made him as if he had been born an heir to his benefactor.

We can define adoption in a spiritual sense as *God's gracious admission of strangers and aliens into the state, relation and enjoyment of all the privileges of children through Jesus Christ.* This is in accordance with that glorious promise of the new covenant: 'I will be a Father to you, and you shall be my sons and daughters, says the LORD Almighty' (2 Cor. 6:18).

Reconciliation, justification and adoption may be distinguished in the following way. In *reconciliation*, God is considered as the injured party and the sinner as his enemy. In *justification*, our Maker sustains the character of supreme Judge and man is considered as a criminal standing before his tribunal. In *adoption*, Jehovah appears as the fountain of honour and the apostate sons of Adam are aliens from him, belonging to the family of Satan, being children of wrath. In reconciliation we are made friends; in justification we are pronounced righteous; and in adoption we are constituted heirs of the eternal inheritance.

Children of God

The Scriptures expressly declare that believers are the children of God. This is because they are born from above, united to Christ and adopted into the heavenly family. The Word of God uses these different expressions concerning our filial relationship to God to help our feeble minds grasp this glorious blessing. One mode of expression supplies, to some degree, the ideas that are lacking in another. To express the origin of spiritual life and the restoration of God's image in us, we are said to be born of God. To set forth our most intimate union with the Son of the Highest, we are said to be married to Christ. So that we might not forget our natural state of alienation from God and to set forth our title to the heavenly inheritance, we are said to be adopted by him. Therefore, the condition of all believers is most noble and excellent. Their heavenly birth, their divine Husband and their everlasting inheritance all proclaim it. The apostle John, amazed at the love of God manifested in adoption, could not hold back, exclaiming with wonder: 'Behold what manner of love the Father has bestowed on us, that we should be called children of God!' (1 John 3:1).

Here grace reigns. The vessels of mercy were predestinated to the enjoyment of this honour and happiness before the world began. The great Lord of all chose them for his children, that they might be 'heirs of God and joint heirs with Christ' (Rom.

8:17). He did this, not because they were worthy, but of his own sovereign will; as it is written: 'Having predestined us to adoption as sons by Jesus Christ to himself, according to the good pleasure of his will, to the praise of the glory of his grace' (Eph. 1:5-6). The eternal source of this heavenly blessing is the 'good pleasure of his will', and it is communicated to sinners 'by Jesus Christ'. The purpose in bestowing it is 'to the praise of the glory of his grace'.

Inheritors of glory

The persons adopted are sinners of Adam's race. In their natural state these are estranged from God, guilty before him, under sentence of death and exposed to ruin. To be taken from this deplorable condition into a state so glorious is an example of reigning grace. It is astonishing that the children of wrath should become the inheritors of glory; that the slaves of Satan should be acknowledged as the sons of Jehovah; that the enemies of God should be adopted into his family and the destitute have the right to all the privileges of his children, a right that cannot be annulled. By nature we are so destitute and abominable that we are fit for nothing but to dwell with damned spirits and accursed fiends in the abodes of darkness and despair. However, by the privilege of adoption, we are invested with such a character and brought into such a state as to make us fit to join with the saints in light and angels in glory. Only omnipotent, reigning grace could be sufficient to effect such an amazing change.

Invaluable privileges

The wonderful blessing of adoption is heightened in our minds when we consider the invaluable privileges that the saints possess because of it. They have the most honourable character because they are called not merely servants or even friends, but the sons of God. Such a privilege can never be changed (Isa. 56:5). David esteemed highly being the son-in-law to an earthly king (1 Sam. 18:23). How much more should believers esteem being the children of the one who is King of kings and Lord of lords! The dignity of their relationship to God is immensely great. Being the children of God, they have Jehovah himself as their Father and Christ acknowledges them as his brethren.

Bride of Christ

They are also the Bride of Christ. Nothing can be more honourable or blessed than this marriage relationship with him. Christ is the 'chief among ten thousand' and 'altogether lovely' (S. of S. 5:10, 16). When David, though not in possession of the crown, sent his men to Abigail in order for her to become his wife, she bowed herself to the earth and said, 'Here is your maidservant, a servant to wash the feet of the servants of my lord' (1 Sam. 25:41). May not the believer, for infinitely greater reasons, adore the blessed hand that broke his yoke of bondage to sin and Satan, and joined him to David's Antitype, the heavenly Bridegroom, in a marriage covenant that shall never be broken and in a union that shall never be dissolved?

Under the Father's constant care

The children of God are the objects of his fatherly affection and constant care. As a father, he guides them by his counsel and guards them by his power. He responds to their disobedience with a rod of correction and in their distress he feels for them with a heart of paternal compassion. In all of his dealings with them he manifests his love and causes all things to work together for their good. They are the darlings of providence and the charge of angels. Those ministering spirits, who are both active and swift, encamp around them and, in ways unknown to mere men, serve the designs of grace in promoting their best interests.

Eternal inheritance

Nothing can exceed the riches and excellency of the inherit-ance to which God's children have a right by virtue of their adoption. This inheritance is eternal and is bequeathed to them by a testament that cannot be broken. This testament, recorded in the sacred writings, was confirmed by the death of Christ. The inheritance includes all the blessings of grace here and the full realization of glory hereafter. In terms of temporal things believers are often poor and afflicted and yet, the blessings of providence are bestowed upon them according to the wisdom of their heavenly Father as he thinks best for their spiritual wel-fare and his glory.

The apostle Paul says that godliness has 'promise of the life that now is' as well as 'that which is to come' (1 Tim. 4:8). Christ himself says to believers that their heavenly Father knows they need his providential favours whilst they continue in this world (Matt. 6:25-34). All things, whether temporal, spiritual or eternal, whether things present or things to come, belong to the child of God. This is confirmed by Paul: 'All things are yours: whether Paul or Apollos or Cephas, or the world or life or death, or things present or things to come — all are yours' (1 Cor. 3:21-22). Elsewhere the Apostle says that believers are 'heirs of God and joint heirs with Christ' (Rom. 8:17). This is beyond our comprehension! Every child of God has the right to say, 'Jehovah himself is my reward, my portion and my inheritance.'

God's inheritance

At the same time, God regards his people as his inheritance: 'The Portion of Jacob is not like them, for he is the Maker of all things, and Israel is the tribe of his inheritance; the LORD of hosts is his name' (Jer. 10:16). All the awesome and adorable attributes of God will appear glorious in the children of God and will be enjoyed by them to their everlasting honour and unspeakable happiness. What more can the heart of man desire? What good thing will God withhold from those for whom he gave his Son, to whom he gives himself?

Given the Spirit of adoption

As a testimony to this wonderful relationship and as a sign of his promise of their future inheritance, the children of God receive the 'Spirit of adoption' by whom they cry out with confidence, 'Abba, Father' (Rom. 8:15). The Spirit of adoption, as opposed to the spirit of bondage, is the Spirit of light and liberty, of comfort and joy. He glorifies Christ in the believer's sight and sheds the love of God abroad in his heart. The Spirit reminds him of the promises of God and enables him to plead them at the throne of grace. He elevates the affections to love heavenly things and seals him, as an heir of the kingdom, to the day of redemption. The fact that grace reigns makes the privileges of God's adopted sons sure and certain.

We would regard it as a great mercy to obtain the least favour from the eternal King. What an honour to be the lowest servant of the God of heaven! Yet, as believers we are his adopted children and he, the Fountain of all bliss and Maker of all things, is our everlasting Father. We are his espoused bride and he, the Sovereign of all worlds and object of angelic worship, is our Husband. What rich blessings to bestow upon sinful mortals who can say to corruption, 'You are my father' and to the worm, 'You are my mother and my sister' (Job 17:14). How amazing that we should be permitted to say to the infinite God, 'You are our portion: All that you have and all that you are belong to us, to make us completely happy and eternally blessed.' We can conceive of no greater or more glorious blessing to be enjoyed.

Eternal riches

Let the rich and famous boast about their lavish lifestyle. The poorest believer in Christ is superior to them all. Though they wear expensive clothing and jewels; though their names are held in the highest esteem by men of the world; though worldly riches pour continually into their laps; yet they must soon, with everyone else, 'lie down alike in the dust, and worms cover them' (Job 21:26). Their memory shall rot but the new name of the weakest Christian is everlasting (Prov. 10:7). It may be neglected and despised by men but it shall stand for ever fair in the book of life. You may not be distinguished as an important person nor receive the acclamations of the people but, as you proceed on your pilgrimage in the vale of life, you are regarded highly in heaven and the most wonderful honours are yours.

Your praise is not of men but of God. He knows the way that you take and commands the angels to consider you as the object of their care. You may not be able to boast of famous ancestors or of noble blood but, being born from above, the royal blood of heaven runs in your veins. You may not be intimately acquainted with an earthly king or queen but, like a prince, you have power with the God of Israel. You may not be very well off in material things but the unsearchable riches of Christ are all your own. You may not have numerous servants to attend you and you may live in a very humble abode, but the holy angels guard you and serve your interests and the God of glory condescends to dwell with you under your humble roof.

How honourable and happy is your spiritual state! Abundant wealth could not buy such happiness. Earthly monarchs cannot confer such honour. The Lord of hosts has purposed to bring down the pride of all other glory but this honour shall never be laid in the dust. It puts all fleeting, worldly honour into the shade. How encouraging it is to reflect on the lasting and exalted happiness of the sons of God! Christianity! It is your role to make the human mind noble and truly great. Grace! It is your role to raise the poor from the dunghill and the needy out of the dust; to number them among the princes of heaven and to seat them on thrones of glory.

In conclusion

What is your spiritual condition? If you are a real Christian, you are a child of God and an adopted heir of everlasting glory. Do you know by experience the privileges connected with such an honour? If not, you are a Christian in name only. In fact, far from being a Christian, you are an enemy of God and a child of the devil. Are you prepared to believe this or will your pride be offended at it? All mankind can be divided into the children of God and the children of the devil. Where do you consider yourself to be?

Be content

Are you a believer? That is, are you a child of God by adoption and an heir of eternal riches? Be diligent in living up to your high character and exalted privileges. Let the children of this world satisfy their little minds and be captivated by the low enjoyments and perishing vanities of the present state; you should disdain acting upon their principles and being governed by their maxims. The riches of the world, which engross the cares of the covetous; its honours, which are so earnestly pursued by the ambitious; and its many pleasures, in which the sensual person delights, should hold no attraction for you. Why should you feel discontented because you do not have the things that cannot make you happy, even if you were to enjoy them to the full? Furthermore, you should not perform religious duties out of the same motives as the legal moralist and selfish Pharisee. Such a person either seeks the applause of men, which is sheer hypocrisy in the sight of the one who searches the heart, or seeks to gain acceptance with God, which seriously usurps the office of Christ and brings dishonour upon his work. Such a person supposes that the work of the Lord is not perfect in itself or not freely available to the sinner. In both cases the Redeemer is far from being honoured in his wonderful office as Saviour. The children of light should act out of the purest motives of love to their heavenly Father and gratitude to the Saviour who shed his blood in order to glorify God.

Be in *the world, not* of *it*

Are you an heir of the kingdom? You should watch over your conduct in the church of God and in the world. Your zeal for your Father's honour should not be by 'fits and starts' but should affect the way that you live all of the time. Seek to show that you are a diligent servant, as well as a dignified son of God. Your lifestyle should be, as much as possible, in agreement with your holy profession and your glorious hope. Your heart and conduct should be in heaven because that is where your gracious Father and loving Husband, your brothers and sisters in Christ and your bright inheritance all dwell.

Although you are heir of a kingdom, it is not of this world (John 18:36). Though you are in the world, you are not of the world. Therefore, you should not be surprised or ashamed if the world hates you. The children of God must, above all others, take to heart the words of the apostle Paul: 'Whatever things are true, whatever things are noble, whatever things are just, whatever things are pure, whatever things are lovely, whatever things are of good report, if there is any virtue and if there is anything praiseworthy — meditate on these things' (Phil. 4:8).

No one can free himself from the terrible charge of bringing dishonour upon Christ and reproach upon Christianity, if he lives under the dominion of sin and is a servant of Satan. Such a person may have a head knowledge of the doctrine of grace and may even profess a love for it, but he is without the true faith of the gospel and is an enemy to the cross of Christ. He puts a stumbling block in the way of young believers and, if he leaves the world in this condition, he will pay a severer penalty and will fall under double condemnation to all eternity.

The reign of grace

Chapter 8

The reign of grace in our sanctification

'The very grace which
provides, reveals and
applies the blessings of
salvation also teaches,
motivates and sweetly
constrains a believer to
deny himself and to walk
in ways of holiness.'

8.
The reign of grace in our sanctification

We have considered how the relationship of the sinner to God changes because of justification and adoption. I now want to consider the change that takes place within the heart of the sinner. This change is real and is an absolute necessity. It begins in sanctification and is made perfect in glory.

It is true that Christ is proclaimed freely to sinners in the gospel and that when the obedience of Christ is imputed to us for our justification we are considered as ungodly. Yet, before we can enter the mansions of endless purity, we must be sanctified. Indeed, Christ finds his people completely destitute of holiness and of any desires for it, but he does not leave them in such a condition. He produces in them a sincere love to God and a real pleasure in his ways. Believers are called a 'holy nation' (1 Peter 2:9). Holiness is the health of the soul and the beauty of a rational nature. It is the glory of the church of God and is essential to true happiness. For these reasons, in a treatise on reigning grace, sanctification must not be overlooked. We may be sure that grace reigns in it.

Sanctification is of vast importance in the plan of grace. It is the end of our eternal election; a wonderful promise and blessing of the covenant of grace; a precious fruit of redemption by the blood of Jesus; the purpose of God in regeneration; the primary intention of justification; the scope of adoption and an absolute necessity to glorification. In the sanctification of a sinner all of God's glorious works in redemption are united.

Therefore, sanctification may be justly regarded as a wonderful part of our salvation. This is far better than calling it a condition of salvation. To be delivered from bondage to sin and Satan and to be renewed in the image of God must certainly be esteemed as a great deliverance and a valuable blessing. The very essence of sanctification is to enjoy this deliverance and share in this blessing. Therefore, we can define sanctification as the *work of God's grace by which those that are called and justified are renewed in the image of God.*

Effects of sanctification

Love for God

The effect of this glorious work is true holiness or conformity to the moral perfections of the deity; in other words, love to God and delight in him as the chief Good. 'The purpose of the commandment is love from a pure heart' (1 Tim. 1:5). To love the Supreme Being is directly contrary to the bias of corrupt nature. As natural depravity consists in our aversion to God, which reveals itself in numerous ways, so the essence of true holiness consists in love to God. This heavenly affection is the fruitful source of all obedience to him and all delight in him, both here and hereafter. Love to God is also the sum and perfection of holiness. All acceptable works flow from this love and are the necessary expressions of it.

Changed life

Justification and sanctification are both blessings of grace and are absolutely inseparable. Yet, they are distinct and in various ways are quite different. Justification is a legal action which, in a single act of grace, brings freedom from punishment and a right to eternal life. Sanctification is a continual work of grace within the heart that results in a real change taking place in the manner of life. Justification takes place because of a righteousness outside of us. Sanctification is holiness wrought within us. The latter will always, without exception, follow the former. In justification Christ acts as a priest in removing the guilt of sin; in sanctification he acts as a king in subduing the dominion of sin. In one, the condemning power of sin is removed; in the other, the reigning power of sin is removed. Justification is instantaneous and complete, but sanctification is progressive and perfected by degrees.

Obedient to his ways

The people on whom the blessing of sanctification is bestowed are those who are justified and accepted by God. In the language of reigning grace, it is written of them: 'I will put my law in their minds, and write it on their hearts' (Jer. 31:33). The blessing promised is a love to God and delight in his law and ways. These things are implanted in the hearts of all the regenerate, which constantly inclines them to obey the whole revealed will of God as far as they know it. Sanctification is a new covenant blessing and in this gracious arrangement it is promised as a special privilege. It is clearly not required as a condition which entitles the believer to God's blessing.

Acceptance with God

Those happy souls who know the blessing of being delivered from sin's dominion are 'not under law but under grace' (Rom. 6:14). This means that they do not need to seek to be justified by keeping the law nor are they under the curse of the law. They are completely justified by the free favour of God and live under its powerful influence. This text strongly implies that those who are under the law, as a covenant, or who are seeking

acceptance with God by their own works, are under the dominion of sin, however well thought of they might be by others and
whatever claims they make concerning themselves. Those who
are under the law have no real holiness nor can they do anything that is acceptable to God. 'Those who are in the flesh
cannot please God' (Rom. 8:8). Those who are under the law
are condemned by it and whatever they do, whilst in this state,
cannot be accepted. A man's person must be accepted by God,
before his works can be pleasing to him.

What is a good work?

To make all this clearer, it might be useful to consider that
for a work to be truly good, it must have three particular
characteristics.

1. *It must be done from a right principle.* This is the love of
God. The great command of the unchangeable law is, 'You
shall love the LORD your God' (Mark 12:30). Whatever work is
done from any other principle, however much applauded by
men, is not acceptable in the sight of the one who searches the
hearts. God weighs principles as well as actions.

2. *It must be performed by a right rule.* This is the revealed will
of God that is the rule of righteousness. The moral law, in particular, is the rule of our obedience. It is a complete system of
duty and, as moral law, is the unchanging rule of our conduct.
A person may regard his works as very commendable and may
be very diligent in performing them, but if they are not commanded by the authority of heaven, they stand condemned by
that divine question, 'Who has required this from your hand?'
(Isa. 1:12). Those who are deceived by superstition claim, as
they have always done, that their works have the love of God
as the principle and the glory of God as the end. But if what

they do is not enjoined in Scripture, as the only rule of faith and practice, it is worthless and will certainly be rejected by God. Where there is no command, explicit or implied, there can be no obedience and consequently no good work.

3. *It must also be intended for a right end.* This is the glory of the Supreme Being. 'Whatever you do, do all to the glory of God' (1 Cor. 10:31). This is the command of the Most High, which is binding upon us at all times. This is the end for which Jehovah works both in providence and grace and is the highest end at which we can possibly aim. However, no man can act for so sublime an end but he that is taught by God that justification is entirely by grace and not by any conditions performed by him. Until a man has learned this, he will always think of his supposed good works as gaining acceptance with God. Men may do good things for this and many other reasons but works which are truly good, which the Holy Spirit calls the 'fruits of righteousness', are intended by the believer to be 'to the glory and praise of God' (Phil. 1:11).

An unregenerate man may do many things that are good in themselves and even by a right rule. But those who are ignorant of the gospel of God's grace cannot act out of a principle of love to God nor for such an exalted end as the glory of God. These are absolutely necessary for a work to be constituted as good.

To confirm and illustrate these things we must observe that man is a fallen creature, entirely destitute of the holy image and love of God. Far from loving his Maker and delighting in his ways, he is an enemy to God. The language of such a man's heart is revealed by those evil wretches in the book of Job when they say to God, 'Depart from us, for we do not desire the knowledge of your ways. Who is the Almighty, that we should serve him? And what profit do we have if we pray to him?' (Job 21:14-15).

Furthermore, it is impossible for the holy commands of God's law and the vengeance threatened against disobedience to stir the smallest degree of love to God in our hearts. We are apostate creatures and are under God's curse. The purer God's law is, the more contrary it is to our own biased and corrupted natures. It is obvious that those under the condemning power of the law cannot delight in its holy demands. Whilst we continue in this deplorable condition we cannot love the divine Lawgiver as we should.

Belief in the gospel

Fallen man can only love God as he is revealed in a Mediator. He must behold his Maker's glory in the face of Jesus Christ, before he can love him, or have the least desire to promote his glory. As there is no revelation of the glory of God in Christ but by the gospel and we cannot behold it except by faith, it must follow that no one can sincerely love God and desire to glorify him, whilst ignorant of the truth. As the brightest display of all divine perfections are in Jesus Christ and the gospel reveals him in his glory and beauty, so through the sacred influence of the Holy Spirit, sinners behold the infinite loveliness and transcendent glory of God, in the person and work of Immanuel. The gospel is a declaration of the perfect forgiveness which is with God and of the wonderful salvation which is by Christ. Therefore, whoever believes the gospel enjoys, to some degree, peace of conscience and the love of God.

Desire to obey God

The believer's affection and gratitude to God as a being who is infinitely lovely in himself and inconceivably gracious to needy, guilty and unworthy creatures will be proportionate to his views of God's glory revealed in Jesus and his experience of God's love shed abroad in the heart. He will say, 'What shall I render to the LORD for all his benefits towards me?' 'Bless the LORD, O my soul, and all that is within me, bless his holy name!' (Ps. 116:12; 103:1). Being born from above, he finds 'delight in the law of God according to the inward man' (Rom. 7:22). He has a continual desire to be conformed more and more to it as a transcript of God's holiness and a revelation of his will. He now has a heart of love to God and the obedience he now performs is not as a mercenary to gain eternal life as a reward for his work. Neither is it as a slave who is driven to obedience by the goad of terror. It is the obedience of a child or a spouse; of one who regards God's commandment as coming from a father or husband. Being dead to the law, he lives to God (Gal. 2:19).

No one is 'dead to the law' except those who are poor in spirit and who have received the atonement in the blood of Christ by relying on his work alone for acceptance with God. The apostle Paul says, 'You also have become dead to the law through the body of Christ' (Rom. 7:4) He goes on to say, 'We are delivered from the law, that being dead wherein we were held' (Rom. 7:6, AV). In these remarkable words, the believer is described as being dead to the law and the law as dead to him. This means that the law no longer has any power over a believer to demand obedience as a condition of life or to threaten vengeance against him for disobedience, in the same way (to use the Apostle's illustration) that a dead husband has no more power to demand obedience from his wife who is alive or to punish her for disobedience. A true Christian has no more expectation of being justified by his own obedience to the law than a living wife has of help from a dead husband. Also, she now has no fear of suffering any evil from his hand.

Desire to keep God's law

Although the law as a covenant ceases to make any demands on those who are in Christ Jesus, yet, as a rule of conduct and in the hand of Christ, it is extremely useful to believers, even to the most advanced saint. Even when considered in this light, the law cannot lose its authority because it is the rule of obedience that is required by a holy God and which man must obey as he is made in the image of God. To suggest that the law ceases to be a rule of obedience for believers is to suggest that the relationship between the great Sovereign and his dependent creatures no longer exists. It would deny that we are the subjects of God's moral government. To the true Christian, God's commandments are not a burden to be borne.

He delights in the law 'according to the inward man' (Rom. 7:22). As a friend and guide, it shows him how he can manifest his thankfulness to God for all his favours. In regeneration he has received a new disposition from the one who fulfilled the law for him and this gives him a constant and sincere desire for obedience. This obedience is in the 'newness of the Spirit and not in the oldness of the letter' (Rom. 7:6).

If the children of the ancient Pharisees object by asking, 'Do we then make void the law through faith?' our answer is ready: 'Certainly not! On the contrary, we establish the law' (Rom. 3:31). We do so by the doctrine and principle of faith. By the *doctrine* of faith because we teach that there is no salvation for anyone without a perfect fulfilment of all the righteous demands of the law. This is impossible for a fallen and weak creature but was performed by Christ as the Surety. Christ's obedience is placed on the account of a sinner who believes and renders him completely righteous. In this way, the law, far from being made void, is honoured and magnified to the highest degree. The obedience given by the Redeemer to the precepts of the law and his sufferings on the cross in paying the penalty for a broken law, more highly honour the law than the obedience of an unfallen human race and the sufferings which the damned suffer in hell for ever.

The law is also established by the *principle* of faith. As faith purifies the heart from an evil conscience through the application of Christ's atoning blood, so it works by love, that is, a love to God and his people and his cause. This love conforms, at least to some degree, to the law as the rule of righteousness. Therefore, believers are said to be sanctified through faith in Jesus (Acts 26:18). It follows that if anyone claims to believe in Christ, to love his name and to enjoy communion with him but has no concern for his commandments, that he is a 'liar, and the truth is not in him' (1 John 2:4). Our Lord says, 'If anyone loves me, he will keep my word' (John 14:23). The opposite is also true: 'He who does not love me does not keep my words' (John 14:24). Love which does not produce obedience is not love. Obedience is not worthy of the name which does not spring from love. To pretend to love Christ, without obedience, is glaring hypocrisy. Obedience without love is but slavery.

Union with Christ

The great and heavenly blessing of sanctification is the fruit of our union with Christ. By virtue of the union that exists between Christ as the head and the church as his mystical body, the chosen of God become subjects of regenerating grace and are possessed of the Holy Spirit. Jesus says, 'Without me you can do nothing' (John 15:5). Without a living union to Christ, similar to that of a living branch to a flourishing vine, we cannot do what is truly good and acceptable in the sight of God. It is through the Holy Spirit and Word of God that any sinner is or can be sanctified. As it is written: 'You have purified your souls in obeying the truth through the Spirit' (1 Peter 1:22). Jesus prayed that believers might be 'sanctified by the truth' (John 17:19). By comparing these and other passages together, it is clear that God's Spirit uses evangelical truth as the appointed instrument in producing holiness in the heart and life of a Christian. For this reason our great Intercessor prays, 'Sanctify them by your truth. Your word is truth' (John 17:17). Elsewhere he says to his disciples, 'You are already clean because of the word which I have spoken to you' (John 15:3).

Desire to be like him

The truth of the gospel is a mirror in which we behold the all-sufficiency of Christ and his finished work wrought out for the guilty. 'Beholding as in a mirror the glory of the Lord, are being transformed into the same image from glory to glory, just as by the Spirit of the Lord' (2 Cor. 3:18). As the countenance of Moses, after his communion with Jehovah, shone with such a dazzling radiance that the chosen tribes could not look upon it for long; so the believer, in gazing upon the King of glory in his matchless beauty, derives a likeness to that glorious object of his spiritual sight and love. The more frequently he beholds him, the more fully he knows his perfections, of which his holiness is the crown. The more he knows the perfections of Christ, the more ardently he loves them. The more he loves them, the more he desires to conform to them; for love aspires after a likeness to the beloved. The more he loves the transcendently lovely God, the more frequently, attentively and delightfully will he behold him. In this way, he obtains, with every fresh view, a new feature of Jehovah's glorious image. It is clear, therefore, that our progress in true holiness will be in proportion to our beholding the glory of God in the face of Jesus Christ. In other words, a life of holiness to the honour of Christ, as our King and our God, will always be in accordance with a life of faith upon him, as our Surety and our Saviour.

Live holy lives

The fruits of holiness will adorn our lives more abundantly the more we are convinced of the truth of the word of grace and the more firmly we confide in it. This is because the gospel brings forth fruit in those who truly know it (Col. 1:6). By the 'exceedingly great and precious promises' contained in the gospel we are made 'partakers of the divine nature' (2 Peter 1:4). For this reason the gospel is compared to a mould into which melted metals are cast, from which they receive their form and take their impression. 'But God be thanked that though you were slaves of sin, yet you obeyed from the heart that form [or "type"] of doctrine to which you were delivered' (Rom. 6:17). Those that are pressed into the mould of the gospel find that their hearts and lives are conformed, through its heavenly influence, to the law of God as the rule of righteousness. So it is that the truth becomes effectual through the power of the Holy Spirit, to produce that purity of heart which is the mark of a healthy soul, and those good works which adorn a true Christian profession.

Keep the ordinances

The ordinances of grace are not only designed to increase our knowledge of and love to Christ; they are also designed to promote the work of sanctification. Therefore, let all who profess to be followers of the Holy Jesus be faithful in observing them, whether in private or in the family or in the public worship of the church. All who keep the ordinances in faith will find them the happy means of promoting their knowledge of the true God, their growth in grace and their advancement in real holiness.

Incentives from Scripture to sanctification

Let us now consider the main motives that are used in the Scriptures to stir believers into seeking a greater enjoyment of sanctification and abounding in every good work. There are many such motives but all of them are evangelical. For example, believers are exhorted to obedience because they are the 'elect of God' and God's own 'special people' (Col. 3:12-14; 1 Peter 2:9).

What it cost the Lord

The fact that Christ has purchased his chosen at such a high price is a further constraining motive to be holy in every part of our conduct. The price with which we were bought is nothing less than the infinitely precious blood of Jesus, our incarnate God. Any reminder of this should kindle in our hearts the most fervent glow of heavenly gratitude and elevate us to a level of seraphic devotion. This should be especially true as we reflect upon our spiritual condition when the Lord Redeemer undertook our cause and gave his very life as a ransom for us. In the sufferings of Christ on the cross we behold his tender compassion to perishing souls and his intense regard to the rights of his Father's violated law. These considerations must surely move us to put to death our sinful desires and cause our growth in grace; to make us loathe sin and love the law as being 'holy and just and good' (Rom. 7:12).

His compassion towards us

Here we see the tenderest compassion to our perishing souls, expressed in a way beyond the power of language and of our finite understanding. To the astonishment of the heavenly world and the holy wonder of the redeemed, this compassion is expressed in tears and cries, in groans and blood. Consider him, O believer, reproached by his enemies, deserted by his friends and forsaken even by his God. Will not these things fire your heart with holy zeal and arm you with a heavenly resolve to crucify every lust and mortify every vile affection?

The sufferings of the cross

Did Hannibal, at the command of his Father, pledge at the altar to maintain an irreconcilable enmity against the Romans? How much more should the Christian, when standing at the foot of the cross and beholding the sufferings of his dying Saviour, pledge to maintain a constant opposition against every lust and every sin. A consideration of the cross, when applied to the heart by the blessed Spirit, will be more effective than a thousand other arguments and incentives to persuade and prompt to cheerful obedience. Paul was so struck with a view of this amazing love and the righteous claim which Jesus has to every heart, that he regarded a lack of love to him as the highest expression of ingratitude and wickedness and boldly pronounced all in such a condition to be utterly accursed (1 Cor. 16:22).

The keeping of the law

Here we behold the Redeemer's love and regard to his Father's law and government. Christ was determined to save rebels from deserved destruction but not to the dishonour of the law which had been broken. For this reason he obeyed the law's precepts and suffered its penalty. In this he declared very emphatically that the law is entirely holy and good and, in the penalty it demands for disobedience, perfectly just. At the same time he demonstrated that those who die under its curse are punished justly with everlasting destruction. What a noble incentive to labour and strive for a more perfect conformity to the law's holy precepts in your thoughts, words and actions; in all that you are and in all that you do! As you realize that the Lord, out of love to your soul and honour to the law, refused not to die the most humiliating death for your salvation, so you will feel the strongest obligation to love his name, revere his law, trust in his atoning death and follow his example.

The atonement of his blood

The purpose of Christ's redeeming love in shedding his blood upon the cross is that we should serve the Lord without fear, in holiness and righteousness all the days of our life and that we should live for him who died for us and rose again (Luke 1:74-75; 2 Cor. 5:15). Beholding such an amazing deliverance, we say with Ezra, 'Since you our God ... have given us such deliverance as this, should we again break your commandments?' (Ezra 9:13-14). The heart that is not moved, by such considerations as these, to love the Redeemer and to glorify his name, is harder than stone, colder than ice; without any feelings of gratitude. If believers were more fully acquainted with the love of a dying Saviour and the infinite power of his atoning blood, their dependence on him would be more steady and their love to him would be more fervent. They would be more patient in affliction, more thankful, more ardent in their devotion, more holy and more useful. What happiness they would know in this life; what peace and joy they would know in the face of death and a future world! In all these things we see that the redeeming love of the Holy One of God is a noble and constraining motive to holiness of life.

Our heavenly calling

The calling of the believer is also an incentive to holiness of life. 'As he who called you is holy, you also be holy in all your conduct' (1 Peter 1:15). The Christian should often meditate on the nature and excellence of his high, holy and heavenly calling. He is called out of darkness into God's marvellous light, and from the power of darkness into the kingdom of the beloved Son of God (1 Peter 2:9; Col. 1:13). The believer has been brought out of a state of wrath and alienation with God into one of peace and communion with him. The very purpose of this calling is that he might be holy and declare the praises of his glorious Saviour here below and then glorify him in heaven above. What a blessing to be called by God! What a gracious and glorious purpose God has in calling us! To think upon these things must incline our hearts to holiness.

God's many mercies

The mercies of God also attract the heart to holy living. This is especially true of that special mercy revealed in the free pardon of sins and the imputed righteousness of Christ. These things have a mighty influence to draw out all the powers of our souls to live in cheerful obedience to the God of mercy (Rom. 12:1). The forgiveness which is with God, far from being an incentive to sin, causes believers to fear, love and adore him (Ps. 130:4). In a similar way, Paul says to believers, 'Sin shall not have dominion over you' (Rom. 6:14). What is the reason for this? Are believers bound to obedience on pain of incurring the curse of a righteous law? Are they to obey in order to avoid suffering eternal ruin? Far from it. The reason for obedience is this: 'You are not under law but under grace' (Rom. 6:14). Grace is described as having dominion. Grace reigns in our sanctification. Grace is a powerful motive to holy obedience.

Our new relationship to him

The filial relationship which believers have with God and their hope of eternal life are further incentives to holiness (Eph. 5:1; Phil. 2:15). The inspired writers often mention these things in order to promote conduct which is in keeping with such dignity and privileges. Surely, the children of God should act from higher and nobler principles than those who are still slaves of sin. A Christian has been born from above, enjoys the honour of being a child of God and is looking forward to a glorious inheritance.

Such considerations move him to live in a way as becomes a citizen of the New Jerusalem and one who expects to receive an eternal crown. The indwelling of the Holy Spirit which brings assurance and comfort is also used to advance believers in holiness (1 Cor. 6:19-20; Eph. 4:30). The fact that without the Spirit we cannot do anything is a powerful incentive not to grieve this sacred inhabitant by loose and careless living.

The promises of Scripture

The great and precious promises of Scripture provide further motives to induce God's children to press forward after holiness of heart and life (2 Peter 1:4; 2 Cor. 7:1). As Peter says, by the influence of these promises on the soul, we are made 'partakers of the divine nature'. How glorious are these promises that Jehovah himself has made!

His loving chastisement

The chastisements with which the Lord, as a Father, corrects his children when they go astray is yet another motive to stir them up to follow holiness and to make them resist temptation. We must observe the distinction between a loving father correcting his children on account of disobedience and a judge who condemns the guilty to a particular punishment. The Lord acts in the former sense and not the latter towards the heirs of glory. When their heavenly Father chastises, it is to correct for faults committed and is done in love rather than in wrath. He does this so that they become 'partakers of his holiness' and that they 'may not be condemned with the world' (Heb. 12:10; 1 Cor. 11:32). Though the Lord's chastisements may be severe and grievous at times, they are still the fruit of his fatherly care and have a glorious purpose. He will correct his children but never disinherit them. He will make them smart for their folly but will not abandon them to ruin (Ps. 89:30-33). As the Lord corrects his children when disobedient, so he reveals more of his love to those who walk consistently in the paths of duty. Those who keep up the closest communion with him and obey eagerly his commandments have every reason to expect richer manifestations of his love; to live more under the smiles of his countenance and to be more joyful in their earthly pilgrimage, having larger foretastes of future glory. However, those who backslide more frequently and who are not so careful to keep God's Word will be corrected more often by him and thus find their happy fellowship with him broken.

It must be confessed that this motive to holiness is less pure and gracious than those already mentioned. However, it does have its use in this present imperfect state. It is also based upon a principle of holy love for God. Though the redeemed of the Lord fear the frowns of their Father's face and the lashes of his correcting rod, yet they do not live under a slavish dread of eternal wrath. Neither are they kept in the way of duty by tormenting fears of that awful punishment. They may expect greater manifestations of their Father's love when they walk in obedience to him, yet they do not obey to obtain life or to gain a right of inheritance.

No, they are already heirs. They are not only servants but sons, and they have a filial affection for the one who has given them new life and a living hope. Although this motive is not so pure and noble as those mentioned previously, which are based upon blessings *already* received, yet this savours of love to God and has a regard for his glory. The obedience performed under the influence of this motive is of a different kind from all the duties of the most zealous moralist, who is unacquainted with salvation by grace.

However, it must be granted that the more pure our views are of the glory of God, the more perfect and acceptable is our obedience in the sight of our heavenly Father. At the same time we must avoid thinking that our best duties are accepted by God for their own sake. Our works are acceptable to God, not because they are perfect or we are worthy but because of our union with Christ and our justification in him. The fruits of holiness are evidences of our union with Christ and are accepted through him, as our great High Priest who ministers in the heavenly sanctuary. They are accepted, not in order to justify us, but as a testimony of our love, gratitude and concern for the glory of God.

I am not suggesting that these are all the motives to obedience with which Scripture furnishes the believer and which he must keep in his mind. These are some of the main incentives to a holy life and if they have their proper influence upon us, it means that we shall not be 'barren nor unfruitful in the knowledge of our Lord Jesus Christ' (2 Peter 1:8).

In conclusion

From all that we have considered, it is clear that sanctification is an important part of the salvation and happiness which are promised to the people of God and which are provided for them. Therefore, consider it carefully and seek after it. Be diligent in the pursuit of holiness, not as the condition of your justification but as the crowning beauty of a rational nature which is made in the image of the blessed God and by which you can bring the highest honour to his name. The perfection of your intellectual powers lies here, and will result in everlasting glory. Although holiness and good works give believers no right to eternal life (this is the prerogative of divine grace through the work of the Mediator), the children of God should always earnestly seek a higher and still higher degree of holiness. In this way they show that they are in Christ and are free from all condemnation.

We have seen that no obedience is acceptable to God unless it is from a principle of love to his name and is performed with a view to his glory. We also know that these things are impossible except to a believer who is freely justified. Therefore, it is quite absurd to exhort sinners to do this or that in order to be accepted by Christ or to prepare them to be justified. Acceptance with Christ is acquired by the sinner but is bestowed freely by God and is the fruit of his eternal, distinguishing love. Indeed, the best works of an unbeliever are but splendid sins. They are not spiritually good in themselves nor acceptable to him who searches the heart. Until we receive Christ's atonement and the forgiveness which is with Jehovah, all our works are done with a slavish spirit and for our own selfish ends.

It is clear from all that we have considered, that it is only the gospel of reigning grace that can reform this sinful world. This is because only the gospel, when empowered by the Holy Spirit, can produce true holiness in the heart and give believers such glorious motives to abound in obedience. We see how important it is that this gospel is known in an experimental way. Only the gospel can cause us to delight in obedience. When we know the truth as it is in Jesus, only then do the ways of wisdom become ways of pleasantness (Prov. 3:17). Faith will then work by love to both God and our neighbour.

Let it be your concern to keep in your mind the many incentives to holiness which the Scriptures urge upon you. Always consider it as your essential duty to glorify God by conduct which is holy and heavenly. Remember that 'you are not your own for you were bought at a price' (1 Cor. 6:19-20). Your whole person belongs to the Lord. Meditate frequently upon the love of Christ and the glory of God which are manifested in the atonement made upon the cross, as there is nothing more powerful to persuade you to live a holy life. The finished work of Christ at Calvary displays the divine perfections most brightly. Seek, then, to obtain clearer views of Jehovah's glory and of your reconciliation to him by Jesus Christ. In doing so, you will have a deeper abhorrence of sin and will be humbled in your own eyes.

Contemplate the bitter sufferings which Jesus underwent in your place and you will be pained at heart for your past and present sins (Zech. 12:10). The more familiar you become with the love of God which was manifested in the redemption of your soul from the pit of destruction, the more it will constrain you to love, adore and glorify your Redeemer (2 Cor. 5:14). As it is the love of God, manifested in Christ, proclaimed in the gospel, experienced by faith, which first fixes our affections upon him, so the more we know of that love, the more our love will increase. We have seen that love to God is the only principle of true obedience. It follows that as our love increases the more it will influence the way we live. Therefore, the very grace which provides, reveals and applies the blessings of salvation also teaches, motivates and sweetly constrains a believer to deny himself and to walk in ways of holiness (Titus 2:11-12).

The reign of grace

Chapter 9

The necessity and usefulness of holiness and good works

'By obeying God's commandments we show that our profession of faith is sincere.'

9.
The necessity and usefulness of holiness and good works

Having considered the nature of sanctification, I shall now proceed to show why holiness is essential for the believer and why the performance of good works is so important.

Love to God is implanted in the heart of the sinner in regeneration. By this work of the Holy Spirit he is enabled to enjoy spiritual communion with the great object of all religious worship. This fellowship with God is in and through the ordinances and is enjoyed with God's people in the church below. It will one day become a more perfect communion in the world of glory. True happiness consists in this fellowship with the Father and his Son Jesus Christ.

Intimate fellowship with God

This is true for believers in this present world and for the spirits of just men made perfect, who know a more intimate fellowship with God in heaven. However, the unsanctified soul is absolutely incapable of enjoying such pure pleasures. There must be a spiritual discernment or heavenly taste, before things of this kind can be desired and enjoyed. As long as a man continues in his natural state of enmity with God and loving sin, he cannot have any real pleasure in approaching his Maker.

'Can two walk together, unless they are agreed?' (Amos 3:3).
Our Lord says, 'Unless one is born again, he cannot see the
kingdom of God' (John 3:3). We learn elsewhere that without
holiness no one will see the Lord (Heb. 12:14).

The holiness that the Scriptures so expressly requires in order
to enjoy God is possessed by all those who are born from above
and justified by faith. All those who are regenerated by grace
love God and this love is the great principle of holiness and the
source of all acceptable obedience. Those who love the infinitely lovely God have, in principle, the holiness which will
flourish and adorn their future conduct and which will shine in
them to all eternity. Such a person not only has a title to heaven
but is also being prepared for it.

Proves our faith

Not only is holiness of heart necessary to enjoy communion
with God but an outward conformity to God's will serves a
number of important purposes. By obeying God's commandments we show that our profession of faith is sincere. Our faith
is declared to be genuine before men. Of course, they have no
way of knowing this apart from our works. Whoever professes
to believe in Jesus and is not concerned for good works has a
faith which is worthless, barren and dead. By living a holy life,
our light shines before men; we edify our brethren; we silence
those who oppose the truth and preserve the gospel from being
reproached by those who believe that it encourages sin. A
blameless life in a professing Christian has often been used by
God to convince ignorant people about the truth by removing
their prejudices, which then leads them to believe for themselves. By walking in the paths of duty we express our gratitude
to God for his blessings and glorify his name, which is the great
purpose of all obedience.

Distinguishes true Christians

The works of faith and love which believers perform will be remembered by Jesus our Judge at the last day. This will be especially true of those works connected with the poor and despised members of Christ and which are done for his sake. These will be mentioned on that awesome day as fruits and evidences of their union with Christ and love to him (Matt. 25:31-46). These works will distinguish real Christians from both wicked people and nominal Christians who were very strict in their duty but who were only concerned for their reputation. These formalists are unwilling to suffer shame for Christ; they are very reluctant to give their money to support the cause of God and are unwilling to help the poor and persecuted members of Christ. These are some of the reasons why good works should be maintained.

We must be sure to understand that neither inward holiness nor outward obedience constitutes any part of the righteousness by which we are justified. They are neither the cause nor condition of our acceptance with God. We have already seen that the righteousness by which we are justified must be perfect. However, our own personal obedience is very defective. This is true of the best of men in this present life. This means that if God were to enter into judgement with us on the basis of our holiness or works, none of us would be able to stand before him. Our most holy inclinations and best works would be found far short of what the law requires, let alone atone for past sins. 'All our righteousnesses are like filthy rags' (Isa. 64:6). Indeed, we need a High Priest to bear the iniquity of our holy things (Exod. 28:38).

Who would dare to say to the omniscient God, 'Search me and try me and you will not find the least sin cleaving to my heart or works'? Would anyone dare to risk their soul's salvation

on the perfection of their works? The boldest heart must tremble at such a thought and the most upright dare not venture his
immortal soul on such a foundation.

In the righteousness of Christ

We find that even the apostle Paul, the great teacher of the
Gentiles, utterly disclaimed all personal worthiness and yet he
was greatly gifted, he laboured in the gospel, he lived a blameless life and suffered greatly for the cause of truth and for the
honour of his Lord. In the light of the Day of Judgement his
desire was to be found in Christ, not having his own righteousness, which is from the law, but that which is through faith in
Christ, the righteousness which is from God by faith (Phil. 3:9).
Christ's obedience alone can support our hope and comfort
our hearts when we think about standing before him who is a
'consuming fire' (Heb. 12:29). This righteousness was wrought
out before we were even born and is the only ground of acceptance before our final Judge. It is the source of all our comfort
and joy in this important matter. If anyone wants to seriously
ask: 'How shall I appear before my Maker?' the answer is, 'Only
in the perfect obedience of Christ which is freely given to guilty
sinners.' However, if the question is: 'How shall I express my
gratitude to God for all his benefits and glorify his name?' the
answer is: 'By conforming your life to his revealed will and by
devoting yourself, in all that you are and have, to his honour
and service.' Therefore, we find that the covenant of grace
provides the believer with peace and joy in the finished work of
Christ and with the opportunity to live a holy life to God's glory.

Why good works are necessary

It is clear that our good works have nothing to do with our
justification and obtaining eternal life. Yet, for many other

reasons, good works are necessary and it is essential that we know why this is so. If not, we shall run into one of two fatal extremes, either legalism or licentiousness. Legalism will destroy our peace, rob grace of its glory and exalt self. Licentiousness makes grace an excuse for sin, hardens the conscience and makes us worse than avowed atheists.

Christ our foundation

Dr John Owen makes this very point. He says that our foundation in dealing with God is Christ alone and the grace and forgiveness that are found in him (Exposition of Psalm 130). He then compares our holiness and obedience, as fruits of faith, to a building erected on the foundation. Therefore, we must rest upon grace alone. Our problem is that we tend to want to mix our works with grace as the foundation. To do so is to destroy the nature of grace. We are then reminded that we must build on the foundation of Christ in terms of our obedience, holiness, duties, mortification of sin and good works. In other words, our works are to rest entirely upon the foundation of Christ and God's grace in him.

Avoid hypocrisy

There is a great cause for fear that this important distinction is not properly understood or considered, even by those who make a fervent profession of faith. It is true to say that there are many who call themselves Christians who know nothing about Christ in reality and who act more like incarnate devils than saints. There are also many who are strict in their duty and who have a high opinion of their profession of faith but who do not possess the holiness and good works which are essential to Christian character. When you see them engaged in public worship or personal devotions they seem very serious, as though they are very concerned about their eternal welfare. When you see them in their families and in their lives generally they are full of frivolity and use unsavoury and careless language. Some of these pretenders to Christianity also attend places of amusements, which in reality are places of vice and profaneness. You may also see them wearing extravagant and expensive garments, whilst their pious neighbours work very hard and yet cannot afford to buy decent clothing. These children of carnal pleasure either do not care about their distress or are content to simply say, 'Be warmed' (James 2:16). Their tables are loaded down with food, whilst the poor among the people of God are almost starving nearby. Yet, such is their love to Christ and his members, that they think it is wonderful to visit them and say, 'Be filled' (James 2:16). When you see them in their trade or business you will find them to be covetous, grasping and oppressive. Their main concern is to lay up a fortune in order to exalt their families. They feather their nests with what rightly belongs to the poor who work for them. They will certainly answer for such greed. Surely the church is defiled and the gospel is dishonoured by such hypocrites. All of these are children of the devil and slaves of sin. Though they profess the faith, they are, in God's sight, on a level with unbelievers.

Beware of covetousness

As for the covetous, those who are devoted to the god of Mammon, they are ranked in God's Word with extortioners, thieves, drunkards and adulterers. Even worse, they are described as *idolaters*. The sin of covetousness is, I fear, greatly misunderstood and overlooked by many professing Christians. Sometimes a person is known to be covetous but is still regarded as a good Christian. We might just as well say that a woman is very virtuous even though she is a prostitute. Covetousness is often regarded as a small and insignificant fault but when we open the volume of heaven, we find it pronounced as idolatry and Jehovah threatening everlasting punishment to those guilty of it (1 Cor. 6:9-10; Eph. 5:5; Col. 3:5; Ps. 10:3).

What exactly is this serious sin? Covetousness, in the language of inspiration, is *the desire of having more*. Therefore, whoever constantly desires wealth is, in the estimation of heaven, a covetous man. This is true regardless of his position in life or religious profession. A man may be rich or poor but if he always desires more, he is covetous. If he is a professing Christian, he will always find a way of hiding the sinfulness of his idolatrous heart. He may be safe from the censure of a visible church but one day it will be fully known where he has placed his affections and whether he has really served God or Mammon. Perhaps there are few sins for which so many excuses are made as covetousness or the love of the world. For this reason professing Christians should guard their hearts all the more diligently against it. It was not without reason that our Lord gave that solemn warning to all his followers: 'Take heed and beware of covetousness' (Luke 12:15).

Therefore, we conclude that he who professes faith in Jesus and yet does not love God and his neighbour has no right to the name of Christian.

The reign of grace

Chapter 10

The reign of grace in the perseverance of the saints to eternal glory

---

'The Lord will keep his people, not because they are worthy or better than others, but for the sake of his own glory'

10.

The reign of grace in the perseverance of the saints to eternal glory

From the preceding chapters we have shown that the state of believers is highly exalted and that grace reigns in every part of salvation. However, the believer who knows his own weakness will wonder how he is ever to persevere in God's way and arrive in glory. He realizes that he has many powerful and cunning spiritual enemies, but no inherent strength to resist them. The world, the flesh and the devil are combined against him. In different ways these assault his peace and seek his ruin. They seek to cause him to wallow in the mire of sin like a beast, or to puff him up with pride like Lucifer. In subtle or more obvious ways, with the cunning of a serpent or the roaring of a lion, they try to bring him to destruction.

Resistance to evil

How little strength he has in himself to resist and overcome them! Indwelling sin, even within the born-again believer, makes his desire for what is good extremely weak. His pious feelings are so inconstant and uncertain that he cannot place the least confidence in them.

These humbling truths are seen in the life of Peter. Remember how he said confidently to our Lord, 'Even if all are made to stumble, yet I will not be … If I have to die with you, I will not deny you!' (Mark 14:29-31). How quickly his courage and resolutions failed! In spite of his boasted loyalty, he could not watch with Christ for even an hour in the garden. He thought he was strong but in reality he was very weak. He trembled at the voice of a simple maid and denied his Lord with dreadful oaths and curses. In Peter we see what inherent strength the best saints have in their fight against the world, the flesh and the devil.

Can such unstable and weak creatures hope to persevere and attain eternal life? Can they really expect complete victory and an everlasting crown when such powerful and crafty enemies continually seek their eternal ruin? Yes they can, because they can do all things through the strength they receive from Christ (Phil. 4:13). They will not only be victorious but 'more than conquerors' over all their enemies (Rom. 8:37). This should not surprise us because omnipotent grace reigns in salvation. The love, power, wisdom, promises, covenant and faithfulness of the Father, Son and Holy Spirit ensures that they will be kept until the end.

The love of God

The love of God means that his people are everlastingly secure. God chose them to life and happiness and therefore his love must cease and purposes be overthrown before they can be lost. 'The LORD of hosts has sworn, saying, "Surely as I have thought, so it shall come to pass and as I have purposed, so it shall stand … For the LORD of hosts has purposed and who will annul it? His hand is stretched out, and who will turn it back?"' (Isa. 14:24, 27). Such is Jehovah's delight in his people that he is said to rejoice over them with singing (Zeph. 3:17).

His love is as unchangeable as himself and is fixed eternally upon his people. Consequently, although the manifestations of his love may change, they cannot perish. So we find the apostle

Paul exulting in God's unchanging love and affirming that nothing in the heights above or depths below, nothing present or future, can separate believers from it (Rom. 8:38-39).

The power of God

The power of God also ensures that all who are born again to a living hope are eternally safe. They are kept by this power through faith to salvation (1 Peter 1:3-4). God's power surrounds them as a wall of fire to protect them and destroy their enemies (Zech. 2:5). Omnipotence itself is their shield and keeps them night and day (Isa. 27:3).

The wisdom of God

As God's almighty power is their guard, so God's wisdom is their guide. The honour of divine wisdom is concerned with the preservation of the saints because if a child of God were to finally perish it would suggest, if not a change in God's power, then a change in his purpose. This would mean that there was something wrong with his original plan. In this world a skilful architect, for example, might have to alter his plans due to a lack of wisdom but this can never be true of God. The Scriptures inform us that God has made his grace to 'abound towards us in all wisdom and prudence' both in forming the wonderful plan of redemption and in appointing the means to see it accomplished (Eph. 1:8). How could this be true if any of those who have been chosen, redeemed and called finally perish?

The promises of God

The exceedingly great and precious promises of God to his people give them much comfort in this matter. For the Father of mercies has declared that he will confirm them to the end and preserve them for his kingdom (1 Cor. 1:8; 2 Tim. 4:18). He has said that the 'righteous will hold to his way, and he who has clean hands will be stronger and stronger' (Job 17:9). He has said concerning his people: 'I will put my fear in their hearts so that they will not depart from me' (Jer. 32:40). Jesus himself says that they will 'never perish' (John 10:28). The blessed God has repeatedly and solemnly declared that he will never leave nor forsake them (Deut. 31:6, 8; Josh. 1:5; Heb. 13:5). The Lord will keep his people, not because they are worthy or better than others, but for the sake of his own glory. 'For the LORD will not forsake his people, for his great name's sake, because it has pleased the LORD to make you his people' (1 Sam. 12:22). These promises, along with many others, are 'Yes' and 'Amen' in Christ Jesus (2 Cor. 1:20). Divine faithfulness is pledged in them and infinite power is engaged to carry them out. Let all Christians rejoice in that these promises were made by the one who cannot lie and that God has added his most solemn oath to them, so that every sinner who has fled for refuge to lay hold of the hope set before him might have strong consolation (Heb. 6:17-18). The promise and oath of God, both immutable, guarantee the believer's final happiness.

The covenant of God

Jehovah's covenant with his people in Christ also shows that they can never perish. This covenant is 'ordered in all things and secure' (2 Sam. 23:5). It is stored with heavenly promises and filled with spiritual blessings. The language of the covenant is that 'They shall be my people, and I will be their God; then I will give them one heart and one way, that they may fear me for ever, for the good of them and their children after them. And I will make an everlasting covenant with them, that I will not turn away from doing them good; but I will put my fear in their hearts so that they will not depart from me' (Jer. 32:38-40).

The stability of the new covenant is asserted here in the strongest terms. This gracious covenant is completely different from the one that was made with our first father Adam, which required perfect obedience in order to receive the promise of life. It is also very different from that which was made with the children of Israel at Mount Sinai. This covenant was broken by them and abrogated by the Lord himself. In contrast, the new covenant has the force of a *testament*. It consists of absolute promises, requires no conditions to be performed by man and is perpetual. Here our sovereign Lord declares emphatically that those within this covenant shall not depart from him and that he will never cease to do them good. We cannot imagine greater security than this. It would be absurd to suppose that God would make a new and better covenant than the one he made with Adam or Israel, a covenant designed to display the riches of his grace, only to allow those within the covenant to lose eternal life and happiness. If the new covenant has conditions attached to it for attaining life then our situation is much more hazardous than that of Adam. Whilst under the covenant of works he was upright, as God had created him. We are now fallen and corrupt. If he could not fulfil the conditions laid upon him, how much less can we who are sinful?

The faithfulness of God

The faithfulness and absolute truthfulness of God give a further assurance of the saint's perseverance. The rocks shall melt away, the mountains shall be removed, the entire earth shall disappear but the faithfulness of God in executing his covenant is unchangeable and eternal. 'The Lord is faithful, who will establish you and guard you from the evil one' (2 Thess. 3:3). God has said that he will not allow his faithfulness to fail. He has sworn by his holiness, by the glory of all his perfections, that he will be faithful to his covenant and promises, concerning

Christ and his chosen seed (Ps. 89:33-36). The true believer will certainly persevere because God's purpose is unchanging, his covenant is sure and he is true to his promises. Rejoice! you who follow the Lamb and feel your weakness. The basis of your confidence and comfort is firm and strong. Stronger than the troubles of this life; stronger than the fear of death; stronger than the terrors of coming judgement. Forsake every fear which holds you captive. The God of power and truth and grace has made ample provision for your deliverance from every evil and for the enjoyment of every blessing in this world and the next.

The merit of his blood

The merit of the Redeemer's blood argues strongly for the final preservation and increases a believer's assurance of it. Is it possible that he who loved his people so much that he gave his life as a ransom for them should abandon them? Is it possible that he who suffered such pain of body and agony of soul and who drank the very dregs of the cup of wrath for them should allow them to be taken from him by the devil himself? Surely not. The very suggestion is absurd and undermines Christ's own character. Will not he who suffered so much for them in the garden and on the cross, even when they were enemies, protect them now they have become his friends through grace? Why purchase them at such cost, only to make them an easy prey for the enemy of their souls? Whilst there is compassion in his heart and power in his hand; whilst his name is Jesus and his work salvation, he must 'see the labour of his soul, and be satisfied' (Isa. 53:11). It cannot be that one soul for whom he gave his life and shed his blood, whose sins he bore and curse endured, should ever perish. If this were to happen, it would mean that after punishing his Son once to satisfy his justice, God would punish the sinner again in hell.

Besides all this, Christ's faithfulness ensures the everlasting happiness of the redeemed. He says, 'I have come down from heaven, not to do my own will, but the will of him who sent me. This is the will of the Father who sent me, that of all he has given me I should lose nothing, but should raise it up at the last day' (John 6:38-39). The elect were given to Jesus and came under his care. He redeemed them and is responsible for keeping them until the last day. To fail in this would be to fail in his covenant obligations towards his Father. Such a suggestion would call into question his power or faithfulness, which is absurd and blasphemous.

The intercession of Christ

The intercession of Christ for his people in the heavenly sanctuary is a further assurance that the saints will never perish. This intercession is based on his perfect atonement for their sins. Though accused by Satan and though weak and unworthy, the intercession of Jesus Christ the righteous must secure their final salvation. 'Their Redeemer is strong, the LORD of hosts is his name. He will thoroughly plead their cause' (Jer. 50:34). The pleas of our Advocate are never unsuccessful (John 11:42). He prays continually that the faith of his people should not fail and that they might be kept from evil (Luke 22:32; John 17:15).

Our ascended Redeemer is not like someone who may or may not succeed in his petitions, but he has a right to all the blessings he asks for the children of God. He can claim them because of the promise made to him and his spiritual seed, having, as their substitute, fully performed the conditions of the everlasting covenant. The compassion of the one who bled on the cross and the power of the one who pleads on the throne make the final happiness of believers certain.

The union between Christ and his people

The indescribable union between Christ and his people also teaches the same truth. Every believer is a member of the spiritual body of which Christ is the head, and while there is life in the head the members shall never die. He who rules over all, with a constant concern for the church, declares to his people: 'Because I live, you will live also' (John 14:19). His life, as Mediator, is the cause and support of theirs. As it is written: 'Your life is hidden with Christ in God. When Christ who is our life appears… ' (Col. 3:3-4). Your life is *hidden*; like the most valuable treasure in a secret place. It is *with Christ*; committed to the guardianship and care of the one who is able to keep that which is entrusted to his hands. It is *in God*; the bosom of the Almighty is the sacred place where the jewel is kept safely. What a happy thought! Jesus, our Guardian, will never be bribed to deliver up his charge to an enemy nor will unholy hands ever be able to steal the jewels from Jehovah's treasure box (Mal. 3:17). The lives of believers are bound in the bundle of the living with the LORD their God (1 Sam. 25:29). The bond of this union shall never be broken or dissolved. 'He who is joined to the Lord is one spirit with him' (1 Cor. 6:17). Christ and believers are inseparable.

The indwelling of the Holy Spirit

The indwelling of the Holy Spirit in believers is another proof of this joyful truth. He is in them 'a fountain of water springing up into everlasting life' (John 4:14). As a guide and comforter, he is given to abide with believers for ever (John 14:16). His purpose in regeneration is their complete holiness and everlasting happiness. In taking up his residence in believers, he gives them spiritual enjoyment; causes them to persevere; guides them through life; and conducts them to glory. The Spirit is the guarantee of their inheritance and they are sealed by him for the day of redemption (Eph. 1:14; 4:30).

The indwelling Spirit not only guarantees the future inheritance, but he is also actually a part of that inheritance. It follows that those who know the indwelling of the Holy Spirit have the assurance that they will one day possess the whole of the inheritance.

The Word and ordinances of God

The Word and ordinances of God are designed to promote the perseverance of believers. God's children are kept by his power through faith (1 Peter 1:5). Therefore, whatever increases and confirms our faith in the great Redeemer also helps us to persevere.

This is the purpose of God's Word and ordinances and we see why it is important for believers to make diligent use of them. In the Scriptures, believers have many precious promises to encourage them; many exhortations to direct and quicken them in the way of duty; many warnings given and dangers pointed out, to keep them from evil; many examples of patient suffering and victorious faith for their imitation, comfort and support when in similar circumstances; and many wonderful descriptions of future glory to cause them to set their minds on heavenly things and to sustain their hope.

The ordinances of worship are compared to green pastures in which Christ's sheep delight to feed and rest and which are designed to nourish their souls and to increase the vigour of their spiritual life (Ps. 23:2). When these are used regularly and properly, believers find their faith confirmed, holiness advanced and hope made clearer. In the ordinances they receive the bread of God, by which they are nourished up to eternal life. We can see how presumptuous it would be to neglect these means of grace and at the same time expect to persevere in the faith.

The chastening of the Lord

Even the chastening of the Lord is used by him to preserve his people. The children of God are chastised by their Father so that they will not be condemned with the world (1 Cor. 11:32).

We have good reason to conclude with Paul that where God begins a good work, he will certainly complete it until the day of Jesus Christ (Phil. 1:6). He who formed the universe is not such an incompetent builder as to lay the foundation of a sinner's happiness in his eternal purpose and in the blood of his only Son and then leave his work unfinished. It will never be said by his enemies that God began to build and was not able to finish (Luke 14:30).

Nobody will ever be able to say that the Lord loved and purposed to save his people but then changed his mind. No one will ever have the satisfaction of knowing that they have frustrated God's plan of grace. Yet, this is the consequence of the doctrine that says that a true child of God can lose his salvation. Not even the devil himself, in all his enmity and pride, would entertain such blasphemous thoughts towards his Maker.

Some objections

Temptation to do evil

In the light of these things, somebody might raise the objection that if the preservation of believers depends upon God, then they need not be concerned about how they live because they are in no danger of falling away. In the same way, Satan tempted our Lord to throw himself from the pinnacle of the temple whilst reminding him of his Father's promises to preserve him as the Mediator (Matt. 4:5-7). Our Lord rejected the devil's suggestion, even though he was assured of his Father's care over him. He knew that it was a temptation to do evil and that Satan's use of Scripture was an abuse of God's Word. In a similar way, the child of God is confident of his perseverance in Christ but also knows that he must walk in God's ways and not sin, presuming that grace will abound (Rom. 6:1).

No need to pray

Others may object by saying that because the saints are exhorted to pray for God's strength and grace to keep them, that their final state must be uncertain. We answer that Christ himself was certain that he would again possess that glory which he had with the Father before the world was made. Yet, we find our Lord praying most fervently that he would receive the fulfilment of the Father's promises made to him as the Mediator (John 17:1, 5). This is an excellent example of assurance concerning our eternal state being consistent with relying upon God's promises and praying for their fulfilment! Whoever thinks that he need not pray to God for preserving grace has no right to regard himself as a Christian but is dead in sin and on the broad road to destruction.

Although the Lord has promised that his people shall never perish, he has not promised that they shall never fall into sin. Therefore, believers must be careful not to provoke the eyes of his holiness and move him to use the rod of correction. The frowns of their Father are hard to bear and they lose much of their spiritual peace and joyful communion with him. Such are the effects of disobedience and God's chastisement. When the children of God are careless in their walk and backslide, they often smart under their Father's correcting hand. We see this in David's sorrowful confessions and agony of soul after his scandalous affair with Bathsheba. In such a condition, believers can have their assurance of salvation shaken and even lost for a time. Their hearts can be overwhelmed with anguish and it is only after many prayers and great watchfulness that they know again the smiles of Jehovah's countenance and the joys of his salvation (Ps. 51:8, 12; 89:30-32). No wonder the Scriptures constantly warn professing Christians against indulging their sinful passions. Not only are there sad consequences for them but dishonour is brought to God the Father and his incarnate Son. The Holy Spirit is also grieved, weak believers are made to stumble and the hands of the wicked are strengthened. It is true that our final salvation depends upon our being in God's gracious covenant rather than our own godly way of life but these considerations ought to make us very watchful against sin.

In conclusion

In the light of all this, let me exhort you to walk carefully and watch and pray so that you do not enter into temptation (Matt. 26:41). Remember that your enemies are powerful and subtle and that you are weak and your best spiritual feelings and desires are so changeable. Sin dwells within you as an enemy and will always take the side of those temptations that come from the evil one and this alluring world. Therefore, 'keep your heart with all diligence' (Prov. 4:23). Diligently watch over your thoughts, feelings, motives and attitudes. Remember that your heart is 'deceitful above all things' (Jer. 17:9). For this reason, 'he who trusts in his own heart is a fool' (Prov. 28:26). These things should cause every child of God to live, as it were, at the throne of grace in frequent, humble and earnest prayer until that time when they shall be out of danger and in glory. Can you be indifferent and careless when the world, the flesh and the devil continually oppose you as a Christian? Dare you indulge yourself in sinful pleasures or slothfulness while the enemies of your peace and salvation are actively seeking your fall, your disgrace and, if possible, your eternal ruin? 'Awake, you who sleep' (Eph. 5:14). Get off your bed of rest and enter the field of battle. 'Be sober, be vigilant' (1 Peter 5:8).

Although the believer is filled with fear and trembling at his own insufficiency and weakness, he may still have strong assurance that he will persevere and know final victory and happiness. He relies on a faithful God as his infallible guide and guard. Remembering his weakness will produce humility and watchfulness; remembering his God will impart peace and comfort to his soul. The Almighty says, 'Do not be afraid … I am your shield, your exceedingly great reward' (Gen. 15:1). He knows the eternal God as his refuge and the everlasting arms as his support (Deut. 33:27). The believer has no need to fear because he knows that if God is for him, then no one can be against him (Rom. 8:31). When the gates of hell and powers of earth oppose him, he runs and finds safety in the strong tower of Jehovah's name (Prov. 18:10).

The true Christian dwells on high with Christ and is beyond the reach of every evil. He is always defended and comforted. Everything he needs is provided. How happy are those who are under the reign of grace! God's attributes, eternal counsels and providence favour them and promote their happiness. So it is that God's grace reigns in the perseverance of true believers in providing the necessary means to make them effectual and all to its own eternal honour and praise!

The reign of grace

Chapter 11

The person of Christ through whom grace reigns

'Both the glories of deity and the graces of immaculate humanity are his, and make him a Mediator who is lovely and glorious.'

11.

The person of Christ through whom grace reigns

The person and work of Christ is a large and glorious theme and deserves our closest attention. He is most excellent in his person as God and man, and his work is absolutely necessary for the complete salvation of our guilty souls.

Christ, our Mediator

Our Mediator's wonderful person is an effect of infinite wisdom and boundless grace. The union of his divine and human natures is of tremendous importance to our hope of eternal happiness. By the union of these two natures, Christ is able to perform the work of a Mediator between God and man. If he had not been truly a man, he would not have been able to obey the holy law nor suffer the penalty threatened by it, both of which are essential to the salvation of sinners.

Assumed our humanity

Of course, Christ had to assume our humanity rather than the nature of angels. The law was given to man and he was required to obey it as a condition of life. As man has broken the law and is now under its curse and bound to suffer eternal misery, it was necessary that Christ should himself become a man. We may suppose that if God had wanted to save the fallen angels Christ would have assumed an angelic nature but, as it was man that God chose to redeem, so it was necessary that this redemption be undertaken in man's own nature. As the Apostle says: 'As by one man's disobedience many were made sinners, so also by one man's obedience many will be made righteous' (Rom. 5:19).

Became our kinsman

It was also necessary that the human nature of Christ, in which he was to accomplish our deliverance, should be derived from our first parents, Adam and Eve. It would not have been appropriate for Christ's body to have been created out of nothing or out of the dust of the ground. If this had been the case, there would not have been such a close union between him and us, so as to lay a foundation for our hope by his undertaking our salvation. To be our Redeemer, the Son of God had to become our 'near kinsman' in order to have the right of redemption (Lev. 25:48-49; Ruth 2:20; 3:9).

The first promise declared that the seed of the woman would bruise the serpent's head (Gen. 3:15). Christ is our kinsman and brother. 'For both he who sanctifies and those who are being sanctified are all of one, for which reason he is not ashamed to call them brethren' (Heb. 2:11). What amazing condescension! The Son of the Highest has become the child of a virgin! The God of creation has become the seed of the one who took the forbidden fruit! He who is adored by angels has assumed our ruined nature in order to obey and die for our deliverance! What words can express and what heart can conceive the depth of such condescension and the riches of grace revealed in all of this?

Was free from sin

Furthermore, it was essential that the human nature of the Saviour be kept free from the moral defilement in which every
child of Adam is conceived and born. Our High Priest had to
be 'holy, harmless, undefiled, separate from sinners' in order to
atone for our sins and redeem our souls (Heb. 7:26). If the
humanity of Christ had shared in the pollution of original sin in
the slightest degree, he would have been rendered incapable of
making the least atonement for us. He who is himself sinful
cannot satisfy God's justice on behalf of another, for by one sin
he forfeits his own soul. Here we see the incredible wisdom of
God in its richest glory in that our Surety was conceived in such
a way as to be entirely without sin. Although born of a woman,
Jesus was completely free of the guilt of the first transgression
and from that inner depravity that is common to Adam's children. The perfect purity of our Mediator's humanity is essential
to our salvation and is frequently and vigorously asserted in the
sacred Scriptures. The holiness and righteousness of his heart
and life are there displayed in the most vivid colours.

Did not share in Adam's guilt and corruption

To gain a better understanding of these things, it may be useful
to consider how it is that we as Adam's children share in his
guilt and the corruption of his nature. With regard to the guilt of
the first sin, we need to see that the whole human race was in
Adam and Eve when it was committed and that Adam was our
public representative. For this reason, Adam's disobedience
became the sin of us all and is justly imputed and charged to
us. In Adam, we 'all sinned' (Rom. 5:12). As the descendants
of an apostate head, we are described as being 'by nature children of wrath' (Eph. 2:3). However, Adam was not the federal

head of Christ. The 'Lord from heaven' was not in him nor represented by him (1 Cor. 15:47). The blessed Jesus was conceived in a supernatural way and born of a virgin. He was not born by virtue of God's commandment to Adam and Eve to be fruitful and multiply, which was made before the Fall (Gen. 1:28). Jesus was born because of a gracious promise made after the Fall, when Adam no longer represented all mankind (Gen. 3:15). Unlike us, our Lord did not share in Adam's guilt.

Our Lord Redeemer was also kept free from the *corruption* of Adam's nature. We derive a corrupt nature from Adam because we share in the guilt of his sin. However, Christ was not in Adam or represented by him, as we have seen. Furthermore, when he was being formed in the womb of the virgin the humanity of Jesus Christ was, by the power of God, kept completely free from contamination (Luke 1:35). In this way, Christ shared in the nature that had sinned, without the least sinfulness of that nature.

Christ, our God

It was absolutely necessary that our Mediator and Surety should be *God* as well as man. Without a true humanity he would not have been able to obey and suffer. To have been only a man, however perfect, he would not have been able to redeem one soul. Even if he had possessed the most wonderful created excellencies, they still would not have been sufficient because he would still be a dependent being. The essence of deity is to be underived and self-existent. The essence of a creature is to be derived and dependent. The highest seraph that sings in glory is as dependent upon God for its existence as the worm that crawls on the ground. In this respect, an angel and an insect are on the same level. Therefore, every intelligent creature, whether angelic or human, having received its existence from God and being constantly supported by him, is obliged to obey him continually. It is highly absurd to think that it is possible for any creature to do more than is required by way of obedience, in order that merit might be given to another or that the obedience of one creature could be imputed to another creature, without exposing the first to everlasting ruin.

Perfectly obeyed the law

Therefore, the righteousness of a mere creature, though highly exalted, cannot be accepted by the Great Supreme as any compensation for our disobedience. Whoever undertakes to provide a righteousness for others must be someone who is not obliged to obey for himself. Consequently, our Surety had to be a divine person because the mere creature is under a permanent obligation to perfect and continuous obedience. Therefore, the gospel meets our needs because it reveals such an exalted and glorious Mediator and Substitute.

The Scriptures reveal a distinction of persons in the Godhead. Jesus is the Son of God and is, therefore, perfectly suited to be our Saviour. In his lowest state of subjection and humiliation he claimed to be equal with God his Father. In the incarnation, our wonderful Saviour took the 'form of a bondservant' (Phil. 2:7). By the same act of voluntary condescension he was 'born under the law' (Gal. 4:4). This means that he freely put himself under obligation to obey the law for us as the incarnate Son of God.

Is equal in worth to our sins

We can also prove that it was necessary for our Surety to be a divine person by considering the infinite evil that there is in sin. Sin is an infinite evil because we are obliged to love, honour and obey the glorious God who possesses infinite beauty, dignity

and authority. To fail in these things is a violation of the infinite
obligation that is upon us. Therefore, sin is an infinite evil and
deserving of infinite punishment. It is clear that we need someone whose obedience and sufferings are equal in worth to the
infinite evil of our sins. On top of this we must take account of
the vast number of sinners to be redeemed and the countless
millions of serious offences to be atoned for. Furthermore, someone had to bear the infinite weight of divine wrath within a
limited period of time in order to reconcile man to God and
bring about his eternal salvation. All of this shows that our
Saviour had to be God as well as man. Of course, the Scriptures contain abundant evidence to show that Jesus is the eternal
Son of God. The names given to him, the perfections ascribed
to him, the works he has done and the honours received by
him clearly prove the point.

Is God and man in one person

It was also essential that our Surety should be God and man in
one person. This is because his work was to act as a Mediator
between God, who has been sinned against, and man, who
has sinned. If he had been only God, he would not have been
qualified to have dealings with man. If he had been only man,
he would not have been qualified to have dealings with God.
Therefore, the eternal Son assumed our nature in order to become a middle person and be able to 'lay his hand on us both'
(Job 9:33). This is why he is called 'Immanuel', which means
'God with us' (Matt. 1:23). He is God in our nature.

Is prophet, priest and king

The perfect performance of all his offices as priest, prophet and
king require this union of the divine to the human nature. As a
priest, it was necessary for him to offer himself as a sacrifice for

sin. Therefore, the Son of God had to become a man because every high priest must be taken from among men (Heb. 5:1). However, he also had to be God in order to have authority over his life to lay it down and take it again (John 10:18). Furthermore, the humanity of Christ alone could not have atoned for the enormous load of human guilt, for which he was to suffer. His death would not have been equivalent, in the eyes of God's justice, to the everlasting punishment which the righteous law threatens against sin if he had been only a man. We rejoice that he who suffered, the just for the unjust, was the eternal Son of God incarnate and, consequently, well able to bear such punishment. Just as sin is an infinite evil because of the majesty of him against whom it is committed, so the obedience and sufferings of our Surety have infinite value because of the infinite excellence of his person. The atonement of the dying Jesus is as excellent as the glorious perfections of the eternal Jehovah!

As a *prophet,* he would not have been able to perfectly reveal and declare the character and will of God if he had been only a man (John 1:14, 18). If he had not been a man, we would not have been able to see and hear him (1 John 1:1).

As a *king,* he rules the hearts of his people, he is Lord of their consciences and he defends them in this dangerous world. Furthermore, as king, he will bestow eternal life on his followers and punish his enemies with everlasting death at the last day. Only as God could these things be true of him. On the other hand, as the King in Zion, he must share in the nature of those over whom he reigns.

Christ, our Saviour

The person of Jesus Christ is wonderful and perfect. Both the glories of deity and the graces of immaculate humanity are his,

and make him a Mediator who is lovely and glorious. May this
Saviour be the object of our trust and joy!

Incomparable obedience

As Christ is a Mediator who has power with God and man, he
is 'able to save to the uttermost those who come to God through
him' (Heb. 7:25). The obedience of such a Surety must magnify
the law and make it honourable; it must be most excellent and
meritorious; it must be incomparably and inconceivably great.
It must be of more value than the obedience of all the saints in
the world, or of all the angels in glory. The sufferings that this
heavenly Substitute undertook, the sacrifice this wonderful High
Priest offered up, must be wholly sufficient to take away the
sins of the most guilty sinner and powerful enough to save the
very worst of transgressors. If Christ's person is infinite in glory
then his obedience is boundless in merit.

Sacrifice of infinite worth

The seriousness of an offence is proportional to the dignity of
the person against whom the offence is committed. Therefore,
it follows that the value of the satisfaction made by the sufferings
of any substitute must be equal to the excellence of the person
who is making satisfaction. All sin is committed against the infinite majesty of God and deserves infinite punishment. The
sacrifice of Christ is of infinite worth, being offered by a person
of infinite dignity. It was the sacrifice, not of a mere man, not of
the highest angel, but of Jesus the incarnate God; of him who
is the brightness of the Father's glory and Head over all creation.
As the infinite glory of his divine person cannot be separated
from his humanity, so infinite merit must be connected with his
obedience and sufferings. In all that he did, and in all that he
suffered, he was the Son of God. He was as much the Son of

God upon the cross as before his incarnation. He was as much the Son of God when he cried, 'My God, my God, why have you forsaken me?' as when he reversed the laws of nature by raising the dead. He was Jehovah's companion when he felt the sword of justice laid upon him (Zech. 13:7). He thought it no robbery to assert an equality with God, even when he was nailed to the cruel cross and died under the curse of a broken law (Phil. 2:6, 8; Gal. 3:13).

Was the sin for which he suffered infinitely evil? The person who suffered is infinitely excellent. Did our sins bring dishonour to an infinite God? A Saviour of infinite excellence has made atonement for them. When Jehovah smote our Surety he considered him as 'the man his companion' (Zech. 13:7). We should consider him in the same exalted way when we believe on him and plead his atonement before God. Here we have a solid rock upon which to stand. In the divine dignity of the Redeemer's person and in the perfection of his work there is an everlasting foundation for our faith that is as firm as the pillars of nature and as immovable as God's eternal throne. Standing on this foundation we may know 'full assurance of faith' (Heb. 10:22).

Satisfied God's justice

Many heretics deny the full and complete deity of our Saviour. Some teach that Jesus had no existence before his conception in the womb of the virgin and so regard him as a mere man. Others think of Christ as a kind of superangelic spirit united to a human body. If we do not ascribe to him all the perfections that belong to God (including eternity and self-existence) we make him a dependent being by reducing him to the rank of a mere creature. In so doing, we take away the sure foundation for our faith. The sufferings of a mere creature, and for such a short time, cannot be accepted by a holy God as a righteous compensation to his law and justice for the sins of innumerable millions of hell-deserving transgressors. It is, therefore, usual to find that those who deny the deity of Christ also deny that he satisfied God's justice on behalf of sinners. In this they are both consistent and (what they wish to be called) rational.

These people must ask themselves whether they are able to satisfy God's justice for their own sins. How can they possibly expect admission into the kingdom of glory by the God who avenges sin, without any satisfaction for their crimes? It is certain that the God who governs the universe is inflexibly just, as well as being full of tender mercy. He has revealed himself as a 'just God and a Saviour' (Isa. 45:21). As he has revealed himself, we must know him and trust in him, if we want to escape from the wrath to come.

The love of God the Father

Let us admire and adore the love of God the Father. This is seen in the gift of his own glorious Son to sinners. Compared with the Son of God all the angels and the universe in its entirety are insignificant and quite worthless. God is so powerful that it is as easy for him to create an angel as an insect. The creation of a thousand solar systems and a thousand grains of wheat is one and the same to an omnipotent God. For this reason, when the Father chose to manifest his love to his offending creatures in some amazing way, it was by giving his only begotten Son who is one in nature and equal in glory with him. It was by giving his Son to be the substitute, propitiation and Saviour of sinners. In the light of these things, how striking are the words of the Apostle: 'He who did not spare his own Son, but delivered him up for us all, how shall he not with him also freely give us all things?' and 'God demonstrates his own love towards us, in that while we were still sinners, Christ died for us' (Rom. 8:32; 5:8). Here the love of God shines in all its glory. The gift flowing from this love is infinitely excellent and the blessings resulting from it are perfect and eternal.

Let us also consider the *condescension of the eternal Son*. It is amazing that he who was in the form of God and who considered it not robbery to be equal with God; he whom angels obey; he whom seraphs adore and before whom they veil their faces, dazzled with the blaze of his infinite glories; even *he* was made flesh, took the form of a servant, obeyed the law and gave himself up to a shameful form of death. It is even more amazing that he should surrender himself to die for sinners, for enemies, and for those in actual rebellion against him! These things prove that the Lord Redeemer is superior to all his creatures in the riches of his grace as well as the depths of his wisdom and works of his power.

In conclusion

Let all the heavens adore him! Let the children of men be filled with wonder and burn with gratitude! This glorious Redeemer is available to sinners and on them his power and grace are magnified. So it is that the gospel reveals the love of God to sinners. However, those who deny the deity of Jesus Christ and reject the reality of his atonement not only obscure the glory of the gospel, they destroy it altogether. Therefore, let us reject all heretical views and be fully persuaded that the Scriptures are clear concerning the person and work of Christ. Let the sad and guilty sinner flee to this all-sufficient Mediator and trust in him as being mighty to save. God has promised that all who come to him will not be disappointed. As a divine person, Jesus perfectly fulfils his offices as our priest, prophet and king. Therefore, let us put the utmost confidence in his atonement and intercession, as our priest; look to him for instruction, as our prophet; subject ourselves to him and expect his protection, as our king. Let us manifest the most fervent love to him, as our Redeemer; give to him the most joyful obedience, as our Lord; and offer to him the highest worship, as our God. Many deny his full deity, reject his death in the place of sinners, refuse to honour him as a divine person and do not accept his righteousness as Mediator. Let these take warning that when it is too late, they will feel their need of his atonement and be compelled to acknowledge that Jesus is 'over all, the eternally blessed God' (Rom. 9:5).

Believer, contemplate with wonder and joy the infinite honour that is placed upon the human nature, in the person of our great Mediator. This nature is in everlasting union with the Son of God. It is seated on a throne of light. It is the most glorious and loveliest object in the whole realm of creation. He on whom you rely, in whose hands you have entrusted your soul, still wears your nature while he pleads your cause. The very body that hung on the cross and the very soul that was exceedingly sorrowful in Gethsemane are now, and always shall be, united with the eternal Word. This union is a mystery that we cannot fathom. It is most wondrous and yet filled with comfort because Jesus is clothed with that very humanity in which he suffered afflictions and trials of every kind and degree. This means that he cannot forget his tempted, despised and afflicted people in this world. In himself he sees their image; in his hands he sees their names. He feels for them and suffers with them (Heb. 2:18; 4:15; Isa. 49:15-16). He can never overlook them or forget their needs.

The reign of grace

Chapter 12

The work of Christ, through which grace reigns

'As the obedience of
the Lord Redeemer is
so glorious in itself, so
freely available to the
ungodly and such a
source of blessing to
those who possess it, the
poor sinner has every
encouragement to trust
it as being all-sufficient
to justify his guilty soul.'

12.
The work of Christ, through which grace reigns

Having considered the person of Christ, I now want to consider his perfect *work*, through which grace reigns and her blessings are bestowed.

Christ's obedience

Grace reigns, says the oracle of heaven, *through righteousness* (Rom. 5:21). My understanding of 'righteousness' in this verse is the way in which the Redeemer, as our Surety, obeyed all the precepts of the law and all those bitter sufferings he underwent in order to pay the penalty of the law on behalf of those who had broken it. Grace reigns through Christ's obedience in such a way as satisfies God's justice. Through this most perfect work of Christ, the tenderest mercy is revealed to poor sinners but not at the expense of Jehovah's righteous threatenings against sin. The righteousness of God, as the lawgiver, is seen because sin is punished in a way that brings true and lasting peace to the sinner. What wonderful grace! How suitable to our needs! Let us consider this gospel righteousness a little more.

Conforms to God's law

The work of Christ is in complete conformity to God's law. Whatever the precepts of Jehovah's law demanded, the lovely

Jesus performed in a perfect way. His nature was perfectly holy,
the motives of his actions were absolutely pure, the purpose for
which he did them was entirely right, everything he did was
without defect. Whenever any law was considered broken,
regardless of the terms of punishment threatened against the
offender, he submitted to it in all its dreadful severity. Christ
was made sin for us; he became a curse for us (2 Cor. 5:21;
Gal. 3:13). Amazing love! He suffered the greatest shame and
the most excruciating pain that the malice of men and devils
could invent or inflict. Most terrible of all was the wrath of God
his Father. His sufferings were comparatively short but we must
remember the infinite dignity of the person who suffered. It was
the Son of God and Lord of Glory who bled and died in shame
and incredible pain. Indeed, all the monuments to God's wrath
and justice in past ages and the endless misery that awaits a
wicked world in the future cannot give us a clearer idea of
Jehovah's justice as the bitter sufferings of Jesus, the incarnate
Son of God.

Unequalled in excellence

The work of Christ is most excellent. This is seen from the way
this righteousness is described in the Scriptures. To signify its
unspotted purity, it is called 'fine linen, clean and white' (Rev.
19:8, AV). To denote its completeness, it is called a 'robe' (Isa.
61:10). To hold forth its exquisite beauty, richness and glory, it
is called 'clothing of wrought gold' and 'raiment of needlework'
(Ps. 45:13, 14, AV). To point out its unequalled excellency, it is
called the 'best robe' (Luke 15:22). It is better than the robe of
innocence with which Adam and Eve were clothed before the
Fall. It surpasses the righteousness of angels in glory. Theirs is
but the obedience of mere creatures; in other words, dependent beings. But this, the highest epithet that can be given, is the
righteousness of *God* (Rom. 10:3; Jer. 23:6). It is so excellent

that the Lord himself seems to glory in it, frequently referring to
it as 'my righteousness' (Isa. 46:13; 51:5-8; 56:1).

Everlasting

It is an 'everlasting righteousness' (Dan. 9:24). It is a robe, the
beauty of which will never be tarnished. It is a garment that will
never decay and clothing that will never wear out. It will be the
same when millions of ages have come and gone. Its beauty
will be as lasting as the light of the New Jerusalem and as
unfading as the eternal inheritance.

Fully completed

Furthermore, it is a righteousness that has already been performed. It is not the righteousness that the Holy Spirit is working
in us now. This righteousness was completed when the
Redeemer cried, 'It is finished!' and gave up his spirit (John
19:30). It is here that many people make a serious mistake.
They think that sinners are accepted by God because of a righteousness which is wrought in them and performed by them
through the help of the Holy Spirit. They would say that this
help was purchased for them by Christ when he died. Such
people can never experience what it is to be truly justified as
long as they hold to such views.

Did the blessed Jesus die in order to do something to assist
us in our weak but willing attempts to save ourselves? No. Did
he shed his precious blood to provide grace for us so that we
might be enabled, through the Spirit, to perform the condition
of our justification? By no means. The righteousness required
for us to be justified was completed by Christ alone at that
awesome moment when he bowed his head in death. Of course,
it is true that the Spirit of grace and truth is given to believers as
a precious fruit of the death, resurrection and glorification of

Christ. This is freely acknowledged. However, the view that says Jesus died to purchase the Spirit, so that we might seek justification by our works, must be rejected. Our Lord himself teaches us that the primary work of the Spirit, in the scheme of grace, is to testify of him and reveal his glory to the sinner's conscience (John 15:26; 16:14). Furthermore, the Spirit of truth only begins to sanctify us when we are perfectly justified. In fact, he begins to sanctify us through the very truth that revealed the finished work of Christ for us! To think differently is to fall into the same error as Rome, which confuses justification with sanctification. Such an idea is contrary to the doctrine of the Apostles, the Reformers and of all their genuine successors, both here and abroad.

Absolutely free

This righteousness is absolutely free. We bless God that this is the teaching of his unerring Word. Some may feel their need of this glorious righteousness but believe that certain conditions must be met before they can receive it. This righteousness was wrought for sinners; designed for sinners; and is freely bestowed on the very worst of sinners. It cannot be bargained for, nor is it up for sale. There are no conditions attached to it by way of moral and religious duties or qualifications. It is a free gift. It is given by the grace that reigns and the grace that reigns only deals with the unworthy. This righteousness must, therefore, be received as a free gift. This means that the sinner who knows he is perishing has the greatest encouragement to rely upon it as wholly sufficient for his justification. Sinner, this righteousness can be your very own. Believe the testimony that God has given of his Son and you will receive it and enjoy the comfort that flows from it. Heaven itself proclaims your welcome in coming to Christ and the faithfulness of God assures you of acceptance as you believe in the Saviour.

Received by faith

The Scriptures teach consistently that this righteousness is received by faith and not through obedience to the law or the performance of some arduous task (Rom. 4:5, 16; Gal. 3:12, 18; Rom. 10:5-9). Faith is the *receiving* of Christ and his righteousness, or a *dependence* on him alone for salvation. By simply believing the gospel, we receive Christ's righteousness, enjoy the comfort of it and possess the guarantee of eternal glory. The sinner who is awakened to his sin and danger is apt to think that he must do some great work in order to obtain the forgiveness of sins and peace in his conscience. God's Word clearly declares to such a person that the favour of God only comes through that obedience which is already performed. Neither is the awakened sinner left in any uncertainty as to how this righteousness is obtained.

The apostle Paul contrasts the righteousness of the law with the righteousness of faith (Rom. 10:5, 6; Phil. 3:9). We learn from this that whoever thinks of doing any good work, as the condition of obtaining eternal life, is ignorant of the obedience that the gospel reveals. Such a person is under the law, considered as a covenant; is obliged to perform it in its entirety; and is subject to its curse as he breaks it. This is true, even when someone acknowledges God's help for assisting him to carry out the supposed condition of life. Scripture actually contains an example of this (Luke 18:11-12). The righteousness of the law and the righteousness of faith are directly opposed to each other and cannot be reconciled.

In conclusion

How glorious is this obedience! Through this work of Christ for sinners the holy law we had broken is highly honoured. God's awesome justice which we had offended is completely satisfied. By this righteousness the believer is acquitted from every charge, is perfectly justified and will be eternally saved. Jehovah declares he is well pleased with this work and the glories of the Godhead shine in it. It is both perfect and excellent. Wonderful righteousness! No wonder Paul desired to be found in Christ and his righteousness (Phil. 3:9). Everyone who has received it cannot but admire and adore the Saviour who provided it.

As the obedience of the Lord Redeemer is so glorious in itself, so freely available to the ungodly and such a source of blessing to those who possess it, the poor sinner has every encouragement to trust it as being all-sufficient to justify his guilty soul. The demands of God's law and justice are truly great and dreadful, but the work of Christ has completely answered them all. There is greater power in God's grace and Christ's work to save from destruction than there is in the offences of the sinner to bring him to condemnation and ruin.

It should not surprise us that the work of Christ should be so effective. It was performed by the Son of God himself on behalf of others. God the Father declares his delight in it and all who receive it are treated as his children. It is the primary work of God the Holy Spirit, as a guide and comforter, to testify to it. Any other righteousness, when compared to this righteousness, is quite insignificant. Indeed, it is viler than dross and worse than nothing. Both in life and death Christians of all ages have gloried in this righteousness as the only ground of their hope. In this most perfect obedience believers are now exalted and the saints in heaven triumph, magnifying in song the finished work of Christ on the cross. Who can reveal all its beauties? Who can show forth half its praise? After all that has been written or said about it here on earth; after all that has been sung about it in the world of glory; when considered as the *righteousness of Jehovah,* it exceeds all possible praise. Those who dwell in heaven must know that their loftiest strains, though expressed with seraphic fervour, fall vastly short of displaying its full excellence.

The reign of grace

Chapter 13

The consummation of the glorious reign of grace

'The great theme of all their songs is the grace which rescued them from the hands of Satan, preserved them through all dangers, supported them through severe trials, brought them safely to glory and crowned them with indescribable happiness.'

13.
The consummation of the glorious reign of grace

As reigning grace is glorious in itself and infinitely superior to everything that is regarded as free favour in this world; as grace reigns absolutely and is forever precious to all the disciples of Christ; so the end of grace is equally glorious: for it is eternal life. Wonderful truth! Apart from his own glory, the great design of God in all his gracious dealings with his people is to bestow everlasting life upon them. Eternal life in Scripture means *an everlasting state of complete holiness and perfect happiness, in the presence and enjoyment of God in all his persons and perfections.* As a sovereign, grace brings her subjects infallibly to this joyful state, through the person and work of Immanuel.

What is meant by 'eternal glory'

To help our weak and finite minds form some faint ideas of celestial blessedness, and to inform us by whom it shall be enjoyed, it is compared in Scripture to the most delightful and glorious things that we see around us in this world. To denote its superabounding delights, it is called 'paradise', in allusion to the Garden of Eden (2 Cor. 12:4). Elsewhere we are reminded that everlasting pleasures are at God's right hand (Ps. 16:11). To signify its grandeur, magnificence and glory, it is called a 'crown' and 'kingdom' (2 Tim. 4:8; Matt. 5:3). As a crown, it does not fade away or corrupt. To show that nobody will enjoy it apart from through the obedience of the Redeemer, it is called the 'crown of righteousness' (2 Tim. 4:8). It is also called a 'crown of life' and 'crown of glory' (Rev. 2:10; 1 Peter 5:4). As a kingdom, it was prepared for believers 'from the foundation of the world' (Matt. 25:34). Those who enjoy this kingdom are said to be kings reigning with Christ (Rev. 1:6; 3:21). To inform us who shall possess eternal life and the grounds upon which they shall possess it, it is called an 'inheritance' (1 Peter 1:4). This clearly shows that only the children of God shall enjoy it because a servant, as long as he remains a servant, cannot inherit. Therefore, we must be the sons of the Highest, by regeneration and adoption, before we can truly hope to enjoy the Father's inheritance.

However diligent we may be in keeping our Father's commands, we shall not receive the inheritance as a reward for our duty, but as something which is freely bequeathed to us in the everlasting testament of our Lord Jesus Christ. Eternal life is a gift that comes to us by way of a legacy. 'I bestow upon you a kingdom' (Luke 22:29). Some writers render these words of our Lord in this way: 'I bestow upon you, *by testament*, a kingdom.' The kingdom is most glorious, the inheritance is completely free to the children of God and cannot be taken from them.

Foretaste of heaven on earth

The heirs of this everlasting happiness are not without some foretastes of it in this life. What is faith? 'The substance of things hoped for, the evidence of things not seen' (Heb. 11:1). By faith they anticipate, to some degree, the joys of heaven. In this life, they receive the guarantee of their future inheritance and rejoice in the hope that they will fully enjoy it. Sometimes they 'rejoice with joy inexpressible and full of glory' (1 Peter 1:8). Whoever believes in Christ is said to 'have' everlasting life, that is, its promise and guarantee (John 3:36). Believers find 'strong consolation' in the promise and oath of God concerning their final perseverance and eternal happiness (Heb. 6:17-18). They live by faith on the dying and exalted Redeemer as their surety, their sacrifice, their righteousness and their advocate. When they see the stability of Jehovah's promise, oath and covenant, they have the greatest assurance that when Christ who is their life appears, they shall appear with him in glory (Col. 3:4).

Separation of spirit from body

The future happiness of believers will be bestowed upon them in two stages. When they die, their spirits will be separated from their bodies and will enjoy the bliss of heaven and then, on the awesome day of the resurrection and final judgement, their souls and bodies will be united again. The unerring Word of God clearly shows that the spirits of believers after death are conscious and enjoy indescribable bliss in communion with Jesus their exalted Head. As soon as the mysterious union between body and soul is dissolved by death, the soul is made free from sin and immediately enters into glory.

For the saints, death is no longer a punishment for sin but a privilege and a blessing which comes from the Lord (1 Cor. 3:22). Death is the gate by which they enter those heavenly mansions prepared for them and in which they shall enjoy such delights that cannot be experienced in this world. No wonder that Paul desired to 'depart and be with Christ, which is far better' (Phil. 1:23).

Elsewhere, the same Apostle, as an infallible teacher of God's truth, says, 'While we are at home in the body we are absent from the Lord' (2 Cor. 5:6). He declares that he would rather be 'absent from the body and to be present with the Lord' (5:7). Now, if words have any meaning, we cannot imagine that Paul was teaching that the soul, when separated from the body, would be unconscious and inactive until awakened by the archangel's trumpet. Yet, this notion is warmly espoused by some. If this idea is true, how can departed saints be said to be 'with Christ'? How can they enjoy the presence of God? Furthermore, it means that those who rejoiced in the light of God's countenance and enjoyed communion with him in this world lost these blessings at death! They looked forward to a heaven of immortal bliss, only to be disappointed! According to this view, the souls of believers must sleep for hundreds of years until God's powerful voice awakens them at the last day. This is not very comforting at all for true believers!

Immediate entrance into heaven

Many references in the Word of God prove that the departed spirits of the children of God enter immediately into happiness. In particular, we can think of those gracious words of Jesus to the converted thief, when both of them were on the verge of the unseen world: 'Assuredly, I say to you, today you will be with me in paradise' (Luke 23:43). The thief had asked Jesus to remember him when he entered into his kingdom and our Lord solemnly promises that on that very day they would be together in heaven. Those who believe that the soul sleeps after death change the sense of our Lord's words by changing the position of the comma. According to them, Jesus said, 'Assuredly I say to you today, you will be with me in paradise.' Such an interpretation appears strained and is unnatural and insipid. The thief hardly needed to be told *when* Jesus was speaking to him. 'Today' was Jesus' answer to the petition of the dying thief, who had asked to be remembered *when* Jesus had come into his kingdom.

Unending pleasure of Christ's company

The spirits of the saints enjoy inconceivable pleasures as they dwell in the eternal mansions and abide at the source of all happiness. They are completely released from all troubles of every kind; from all sins and sufferings; from all temptations and sorrows. Moral evil and its consequences are eternally banished from those bright abodes. The people who dwell there are perfect in righteousness and will never be able to say, 'I am sick' (Isa. 33:24). Their garments are always white and their harps are always tuned. They are with Christ and, according to his promise, they behold his glory and are delighted with his beauty (John 17:24).

The infinite excellencies of Jesus, the incarnate Jehovah, are brightly displayed in that exalted state. Those divine and mediatorial perfections, which we see but dimly in this life, beam forth on the holy and happy spirits in a blaze of glory. With adoring gratitude and pleasing astonishment, they reflect: 'This is *he* that once cried as a babe in the stable at Bethlehem! This is *he* who lived in poverty and sorrow and who went around doing good! This is *he* who died that shameful and agonizing death at Calvary to accomplish our salvation!' How must their souls be filled with ecstatic bliss to see their glorified Husband and Head face to face!

Sharing in his glory

The saints are no mere spectators of Christ's glorious exaltation. Whilst they behold their beloved and enjoy him, he entertains and rejoices over them as his friends and brethren, as his bride and portion. On earth Jesus treated his disciples with familiarity. Although he was their sovereign Lord and required deep respect, he did not keep them at a distance but dealt with them as friends. There can be no doubt that in heaven he treats

all his disciples in the same intimate way. He does not keep
them at a distance but takes them into his own state of exaltation. Christ is not exalted above all blessing and praise merely
for his own sake but as the head of a numerous family and as
the Saviour of his people. There is the closest possible union
between Jesus and his people. The head cannot be glorified
without the rest of the family sharing in that glory. Therefore,
believers must be exalted with Christ. Beholding his infinite glory,
their adoring wonder is increased. This does not, however,
diminish their nearness to and delight in him. On the contrary,
their joy is increased as they find that he still treats them as
intimate friends and is willing to generously bestow his glory
upon them.

In this world the saints discern the glory of God in creation
and providence. The gospel affords brighter displays of that
glory because it reveals the grace and love of Jehovah in giving
the Saviour to die on the cross. But in the world to come, when
their intellectual powers have been abundantly strengthened,
they will have such manifestations of his infinite excellence that
will make all previous discoveries of it seem poor and weak.
For they will be surrounded with the riches of God's glory for
evermore.

Beholding the power of God

We find that Paul was enraptured even with the more obscure
manifestations of God's glory. In considering the gospel, he
exclaimed: 'Oh, the depth of the riches both of the wisdom and
knowledge of God!' (Rom. 11:33). In the light of this, what
must it be for the perfect spirits of departed saints to have the
counsels of heaven opened to them? What pleasure they must
have in contemplating the power of God combined with his
wisdom and goodness! How delightful it must be to behold in
glory that power which brought the universe into being and

which sustained it from the beginning; the power that turned the mighty wheels of providence in every age of the world's history; the power that on numerous occasions restrained legions of evil spirits from carrying out their wicked schemes in the world; the power that overcame the hard hearts of rebellious creatures and made them willing to accept salvation in the appointed way; and which, having formed their hearts anew, preserved them through the many dangers that lay on their way to heaven and brought them safely to glory!

Overwhelmed by an appreciation of the love of God

If the power of God is so delightful for the inhabitants of heaven to behold, what overflowing joy must the sight of his love afford! Just as love is the noblest passion of the human breast, so it is the brightest beam of the Godhead that ever shone through the wide creation. 'God is love' (1 John 4:8, 16). The happy spirits in heaven know the reality of these words. They no longer learn the love of God from his names and works because they behold his love in the essence of his being. They enjoy a discovery of God's love as never before. Their immortal spirits are now invigorated and enlarged in order to take in more copious views and receive larger manifestations of divine love than they could possibly enjoy before. They have now traced the streams up to the eternal fountain; the beams, to the very sun of love.

The bosom of their Father, where the thoughts of love were lodged from everlasting, and where its noble designs were formed, is laid open to their view. Now they see clearly why the Son of God became incarnate and why he died the most painful and shameful death, a spectacle to men and angels, in order to redeem them. Their wondering souls view God's plan of grace and realize, with warmest gratitude, why they were not made eternal monuments of divine justice. They see why their natural enmity against God was subdued and why their enormous crimes were pardoned. Everything is traced to the free, distinguishing love of God. With ecstatic delight, their adoring souls behold the love of God as the grand and original cause of their salvation. Of course, such experiences of exalted bliss can only be known in heaven itself.

Understand the vileness of sin

It might be thought that the justice of God, as revealed in the damnation of millions of apostate angels and sinful men, might take away from the joy of believers in glory. Unbelievers raise many objections against eternal punishment and even call the Book of God to account for its clear teaching on this subject. However, to those in heaven, sin appears in the clearest possible light, as an infinite evil that justly deserves unending misery. Their holy wills are now perfectly conformed to the will of God, in full agreement with his sentence upon the offenders and rejoice in its execution on them, whether they are angels or men.

Delight in God's holiness

They now discover more fully how holiness in the Lawgiver, the demands of his law and the rights of his justice were all displayed and perfectly satisfied in the redemption of their souls by the blood of the cross. This is an inexhaustible source of wonder and joy to them.

Furthermore, they contemplate the holiness of God with supreme delight. God is 'glorious in holiness' (Exod. 15:11). This perfection of the Godhead has often been celebrated by the saints on earth (1 Sam. 2:2; Ps. 30:4; 97:12). Now, if those who dwell in houses of clay, and whose views are, at best, very feeble, are so affected by meditating on it, what must be the experience of those who behold it in glory? With adoring hearts and enraptured eyes, with burning devotion and notes divinely sweet, they join the heavenly choir in that seraphic hymn: 'Holy, holy, holy is the LORD of hosts; the whole earth is full of his glory!' (Isa. 6:3). What inconceivable pleasure and joy!

If the face of Moses shone with unusual brightness following his intimate communion with God on Mount Sinai, how much greater must be the radiance of those who behold him without a veil between! The transcendent loveliness of Jehovah is mainly seen in his spotless holiness. The saints in heaven constantly behold this beauty and, consequently, rest in God as the only object of their love and as the centre of their delight. They realize how just is the command that requires the most perfect love to God because of his own infinite loveliness and all-surpassing excellence.

Being favoured with a more perfect knowledge of God and a more intimate communion with him, the love of the saints in glory is increased accordingly. They understand more fully the grace that has reigned in their salvation and this produces a more ardent flame of love towards the Father who chose them and the Son who died for them. All the lovely and infinite perfections of deity shine around them in the light of glory and this causes their hearts to glow with fervent love. They cannot but express their love in response. This love moves them to contemplate God's perfections and his amazing works with ever-increasing delight, which inspires them to be more and more conformed to his image. These delights are nothing less than the joy of their Lord (Matt. 25:23).

Free from the bondage of sin

The saints in heaven are completely free from the pride and selfishness which tarnishes our best services in this world. Now relieved of the imperfections of this life, they constantly and sweetly sing songs of sincerest gratitude and hymns of holy wonder to God and the Lamb, to acknowledge their obligations to reigning grace. They now declare that the only reason they are enjoying the sight of God whilst seated on thrones of glory is because of that grace which, as a mighty, wonderful and bountiful sovereign, reigned through the person and work of Immanuel. The great theme of all their songs is the grace which rescued them from the hands of Satan, preserved them through all dangers, supported them during severe trials, brought them safely to glory and crowned them with indescribable happiness. All possible praise is addressed to the triune God, the 'God of all grace' (1 Peter 5:10).

United with their bodies

Although the blessedness of the spirits of saints in heaven is great and glorious, it, nevertheless, comes far short of that happiness which shall be enjoyed by them when their spirits will be united again with their bodies. God's Word often intimates that the bliss of believers will not be fully complete until the day of judgement is past and the end of the world is come (Col. 3:4; 2 Tim. 1:12; 4:8; 1 Peter 5:4). Therefore, it is right to consider those things that will enhance the happiness of saints.

Raised in glory

The bodies of believers will be raised in glory and reunited to their immortal spirits. This will not only demonstrate God's power and goodness, but also add to their joy. This joy cannot be complete whilst any of God's children continue in this perplexing and sad world, and whilst the bodies of the saints are still in the grave. Even the happy spirits in heaven know that their joy is somewhat lacking while their bodies are still under the power of death. However, they also know that because of the resurrection, death itself, which is the last enemy, shall be destroyed and shall have no further power over them.

The resurrection of the dead is a fundamental article of the Christian faith. It is clear from the Scriptures (and implied by the word *resurrection*) that the same bodies that died shall be raised to life again. In terms of their substance, the bodies of believers will be the same. However, in other ways they will be greatly changed; so much so, that we have no real idea as to what they will be like. This wonderful change is essential in order for the body to be able to enter the exalted state of glory. The Apostle says: 'Flesh and blood cannot inherit the kingdom of God' (1 Cor. 15:50). The present condition of our bodies makes them incapable of bearing the splendour and sharing in the joys of the heavenly world. They could not cope with the dazzling brightness of heaven's glory. Like delicate plants exposed to the scorching glare of the midday sun, they would faint under it. 'The body is sown in corruption, it is raised in incorruption. It is sown in dishonour, it is raised in glory. It is sown in weakness, it is raised in power. It is sown a natural body, it is raised a spiritual body' (1 Cor. 15:42-44).

With these words Paul teaches that the body of the believer shall be made capable of sharing in the praise and happiness of heaven. Our bodies will be raised up by God's almighty power and fashioned by his infinite wisdom into the likeness of the glorious body of Christ (Phil. 3:21).

Conformed to his image

These glorified bodies will be reunited with our perfect and immortal souls. In body and soul the 'righteous will shine forth as the sun in the kingdom of their Father' (Matt. 13:43). The bodies of the saints, being redeemed by the blood of Jesus and made temples of the Holy Spirit, shall share in the joys of that triumphant state. The sufferings to which they were subjected in this world shall be at an end. They shall never grow old and never decay. Who can possibly have correct ideas concerning the nature and excellence of a *spiritual body*? (1 Cor. 15:44). It is beyond our imagination to think of our sleeping dust being raised and fitted for an eternal world by being conformed to the glorious body of Christ. Even the disciple Jesus loved declared: 'It has not yet been revealed what we shall be, but we know that when he is revealed, we shall be like him, for we shall see him as he is' (1 John 3:2). All we know is that when we awake from the sleep of death, we shall be fully satisfied in being conformed to the image of our lovely Saviour (Ps. 17:15). Therefore, we conclude that the resurrection of the bodies of believers from the dust of death will greatly increase their joy.

Public acquittal of sins

The public acquittal of the saints by Jesus at the last day will be a further cause of joy to them. 'Behold, he is coming with clouds, and every eye will see him' (Rev. 1:7). What an awesome sight! Innumerable angels attend him as he comes and gather round his chariot. The brightness of ten thousand suns is lost in the blaze of his glorious countenance. Behold! A great white throne of flaming purity is set up. The Judge, inflexibly just and immensely glorious, ascends the throne and the heavens and earth flee away from before him (Rev. 20:11).

Every human being who has ever lived on the earth is now assembled. The books are opened. Countless thousands of adoring seraphs and anxious sinners await the grand verdict. The wicked, with trembling hands and throbbing hearts, see the horrors of eternal damnation and long to go out of existence. The righteous are confident and bold because the Judge is their friend and Saviour. They appear before Christ clothed in his own righteousness. He cannot reject the plea they make, for they plead the blood which he shed to atone for their sins. Nothing is able to be laid to their charge and so, in the presence of angels and the assembled world, they are honourably acquitted. The sentence of justification, pronounced long before in the court of heaven and court of conscience at the time of their conversion, is now solemnly and publicly declared and confirmed. The works of faith and labours of love performed by them in this world, though forgotten by them, are now brought forth by the omniscient Judge, as fruits and evidences of their faith in him and love towards his name (Matt. 25:34-40). In this way, Christ will number his people among his jewels and confess them before his Father and all the holy angels. Their characters, which were slandered and reproached in this world, shall then be fully vindicated to their everlasting honour and to the eternal shame of all their adversaries. With a smile of divine satisfaction, the Judge will say, 'Come, you blessed of my Father, inherit the kingdom prepared for you from the foundation of the world' (Matt. 25:34).

Ushered into his presence

Having long desired to be near the Lord, they will be invited to come and be with him for ever. In the hearing of the whole assembled world, they will be pronounced blessed of God the Father. In this world they were all poor in spirit and, indeed, many of them were poor in material things. How amazed they will be to be called to inherit a kingdom, just as princes of the royal blood are born to inherit thrones and crowns! They will be lost in wonder as they find that before they had an existence, and before the foundations of the world were laid, the eternal God had prepared this kingdom for them. They shall then be ushered into a nearer and more perfect enjoyment of God than they ever experienced before.

Blessings for eternity

The fact that these blessings shall be everlasting greatly increases the joy of believers. This would not be the case if they knew that at some future point their happiness would come to an end. However, their inheritance cannot be taken from them, their crown is unfading and their kingdom is everlasting. Jehovah himself will be their light and glory (Isa. 60:19). The infinite God is their portion and 'exceedingly great reward' (Gen. 15:1). Therefore, their happiness is as permanent as the divine perfections they adore and enjoy. The inhabitants of heaven know that they shall enjoy God's glory for ever. Indeed, they shall be receiving greater measures of that glory for ever. The deity is an infinite source of blessedness and the finite minds and hearts of the saints will forever be expanding and filled from that ocean of all-sufficiency. How difficult it is to conceive of happiness and pleasure that keeps on increasing to all eternity! Jehovah shall open inexhaustible stores of blessings, as yet unknown to angels, and feast their souls with joys that are ever new. These things are completely unknown in this world among the children of men. Let all the world know that this is the ultimate purpose of the victorious reign of grace! From the beginning to the end of salvation, grace reigns supreme. Surely, then, reigning grace should receive unrivalled honour for all the blessings that believers enjoy on earth and the saints enjoy in heaven. Indeed, grace will have the glory by all the people of God. For when the last stone of the spiritual temple shall be laid, it will be with shouts of 'Grace, grace to it!' (Zech. 4:7).

In all these ways the blessedness of saints will be greater after the resurrection than before it. However, it is important that we are content with what God has revealed concerning the future glory of believers. We should not try to go beyond what the Spirit of wisdom has given to us, simply to satisfy our curious minds. Idle speculations of this sort are pointless and do not build us up in our faith.

The angels will not be standing on the sidelines when the great work of redemption is completed. In this world they serve the interests of those whom God has redeemed. They saw the incarnation of the Son of God and were astonished to see their Sovereign Lord lying in the manger. They saw his life of poverty and reproaches and suffering. They saw his agony in the garden and heard his cries to the Father. They saw him extended on the cross and beheld him laid in the tomb. They were witnesses of his victorious resurrection and they attended his triumphant ascension into the realms of glory. They have diligently looked into these mysteries of infinite love and wondered where they would lead in the end (1 Peter 1:12; Eph. 3:10). They have long desired to see the outcome of the plan of grace and now they do! If they sang and shouted for joy in seeing the creation of the original world, how much more will they rejoice in seeing the world of the redeemed brought safely to glory? (Job 38:7). How they will be overwhelmed with joy to see the bride of Christ perfected in the beauty of holiness and all because of reigning grace, through the person and work of their incarnate Lord! (Eph. 5:27; Rev. 21:9).

In conclusion

Perhaps I could now ask you what are your thoughts concerning these things. It is likely that you hope to go to heaven when you die. If so, what is the basis for your hope? Is your hope a mere wish or is it a well-grounded expectation? The Word of God requires you, as a professing Christian, to 'give ... a reason for the hope that is in you' (1 Peter 3:15). Why is it that you hope to be in heaven, when many millions of others will be punished eternally, especially when the Scriptures teach that comparatively few ever find the way to life?

Delight in God and his people

Perhaps you have never thought very much about these things. Why, then, do you call yourself a Christian? Why do you hope to go to heaven when you have no delight in God; no pleasure in his ways; no love for his people; and no desire for a holy life?

Heaven would not be heaven for you because there is nothing there for you to enjoy. Everything about heaven is contrary to your present inclinations. You do not love heaven, but are afraid of hell. The inhabitants of the celestial world would be no companions for you. Their work would be burdensome and their language would be unknown to you. Their sweetest hosannas would afford you no pleasure; the symphony of their golden harps would sound harsh in your ears. The perfection of God, their highest joy, would cause your greatest anxiety, if you could be admitted to those mansions of purity as you are. True happiness consists in the enjoyment of an object that is completely suitable and satisfying to our desires. Therefore, a holy God cannot be your happiness, without sharing in his holiness. Remember, if you leave this world in an unholy state, you cannot enter the place where purity dwells, but you will be cast for ever into that place where there is 'weeping and gnashing of teeth' (Matt. 25:30).

Build on the right foundation

Are you a professing Christian who is serious in mind and strict in conduct? Even you must consider the foundation of your hope. 'There is a way that seems right to a man, but its end is the way of death' (Prov. 16:25). It is possible to be zealous for God and blameless in life, yet perish for ever. This was true of the Jews in Paul's time (Rom. 9:31-32; 10:2-3). What is the reason for your hope of heaven? Is it that grace which reigns through the person and work of Christ? Can you say with the early Christians, 'We believe that through the grace of the Lord Jesus Christ we shall be saved'? (Acts 15:11). Have you resolved the important matter of the salvation of your immortal soul? Do you have a clear and living hope of glory? Does your hope cause you to rejoice and follow after holiness? (Rom. 5:2; 1 Peter 1:3-6; 1 John 3:3). Does your hope have Christ and his finished work, together with the promise of him who cannot lie, as its everlasting support? You must be certain about these things. If you love your soul, do not be content with uncertainty over such a momentous issue. You are building for eternity; therefore, take care over the materials with which you build and upon what foundation. A mistake in the ground of your trust will ruin your soul. Read your Bible, think carefully about it and pray that the Spirit of truth will direct you into the knowledge of Christ and belief of the truth.

Follow after holiness

Are you a child of God and an heir of the kingdom? Endeavour, through a diligent use of the means of grace in public worship and private devotion, to make much progress in holiness. Remember that holiness is the health, beauty and glory of your undying soul. Watch and pray against indwelling sin; resist the allurements of worldly pleasure; stand fast against the assaults of Satan. Watch against spiritual pride especially. Do not rejoice in your knowledge, gifts, excellencies or even Christian experiences. Be thankful for these things but do not put them in the place of Christ or his Word. Do not make them the ground of your present confidence or the source of your future comfort. To do this is not to rely on God's promise and to live by faith in Jesus Christ, but to admire yourself and to live upon your feelings. The consequence of this is either to be as proud as the Pharisees in despising other people, or to be always downcast and doubting your salvation.

You must constantly believe in Jesus and keep on looking to him alone for salvation. The more you behold the glory of God in the face of Jesus Christ, the more you will see of your own vileness. The more you grow in holiness, the more aware you will be of your inward corruptions and the imperfection of your duties. More and more, you will feel your need of the gospel of grace and you will realize, even after many years of faithful Christian service, that you are a sinner who has no hope apart from Christ. Never forget that in yourself you are unworthy, guilty and condemned; only in Jesus are you accepted. This will promote humility and happiness in your life and will stimulate you to praise God and live for him.

Guard against slothfulness

It is also important for you to guard against spiritual slothfulness. Do not forget that you have many enemies. 'Be sober, be vigilant' (1 Peter 5:8). Time is short and very uncertain. Watch over your precious moments and use them for God. Make sure that the fruits of your gratitude to the Lord adorn all your behaviour. Take the life of Jesus as your example in holiness and usefulness. Remember that the eyes of God, of angels, of evil spirits and of men are all upon you. Your friends and enemies watch you closely. Do not grieve your friends and cause your adversaries to rejoice by falling into sin. Having received the guarantee of your future inheritance and having had some foretastes of the joys of heaven, make it your constant business to live above the world, whether you are in prosperity or need.

Make sure your conduct is appropriate for a citizen of the New Jerusalem in heaven. It is your duty and blessing to live with an eye towards the world to come, as if living in its suburbs. Spend much time with the eternal God in prayer, praise and holy meditation. Cultivate a blessed intimacy with that sublime being whose favour is better than life and whose frown is worse than destruction. By such communion with God, you will taste more delights than all the pleasures of sin can boast and all the riches of the world can bestow.

Through this fellowship with the Lord, you will find his material benefits blessed to your use, your afflictions lightened, your desires for holiness strengthened and the power of indwelling sin weakened. Always try to ensure that, whenever your fair and glorious and heavenly bridegroom comes, he will find you ready with your 'waist ... girded and your lamps burning' (Luke 12:35). If you do, your soul will have peace, your life will be useful and your death triumphant.

While we soar on the wings of faith and holy meditation to explore the wonders of reigning grace, we are raised up, as it were, to the outskirts of heaven. While we endeavour to sound its depths and measure its heights, we taste of joys that are divinely sweet and savour the entertainment of angels. Alas! How soon are we distracted from such holy contemplations by the motions of indwelling sin and the rude interruptions of this noisy, busy and transient world! Yet, for our comfort, we have to remember that after a few more fleeting days we shall finally enter that place where we shall enjoy, for all eternity to come, those infinite delights which flow from the sight of JEHOVAH in the beauty and perfection of his being.

A final word

I conclude this imperfect and brief survey of *The reign of grace* by stating that the free favour of God revealed in our salvation is a theme so extensive and so wonderful that all that can be said by the most eloquent gospel preachers; all that can be written by the most poetic pens; all that can be thought by the most intellectual and sanctified minds, must come infinitely short of displaying fully its glories. After all that is imagined or can be sung, by angels or men, seraphs or saints, in the church below or choirs above, this glorious subject will remain inexhausted to all eternity. For, the riches of Christ are unsearchable and the grace of God is unbounded!